PEACE AND DEMOCRATIC SOCIETY

Professor Amartya Sen is Lamont University Professor and Professor of Economics and Philosophy at Harvard University. He has served as President of the Econometric Society, the Indian Economic Association, the American Economic Association and the International Economic Association. He formerly served as Honorary President of OXFAM and is now its Honorary Advisor. Born in India, Sen studied at Presidency College, Calcutta, and at Trinity College, Cambridge. His previous posts include the Drummond Professor of Political Economy at Oxford University, and Professor of Economics at Delhi University and at the London School of Economics. Among the awards Amartya Sen has received are the Bharat Ratna, the Eisenhower Medal, the George C. Marshall Award, the Brazilian Ordem do Merito Cientifico (gra-Cruz), Companion of Honour (UK), the Edinburgh Medal, and the Nobel Prize in Economics. Amartya Sen's books have been translated into more than thirty languages, and include *Collective Choice and Social Welfare* (1970), *On Economic Inequality* (1973, 1997), *Poverty and Famines* (1981), *Choice, Welfare and Measurement* (1982), *Resources, Values and Development* (1984), *On Ethics and Economics* (1987), *The Standard of Living* (1987), *Inequality Reexamined* (1992), *Development as Freedom* (1999), and *Rationality and Freedom* (2002), *The Argumentative Indian* (2005), and *Identity and Violence: The Illusion of Destiny* (2006), among others.

Peace and Democratic Society

edited by
Amartya Sen

Cambridge

OpenBook
Publishers

COMMONWEALTH SECRETARIAT

2011

OpenBook
Publishers

Open Book Publishers CIC Ltd.,
40 Devonshire Road, Cambridge, CB1 2BL, United Kingdom
http://www.openbookpublishers.com

As with all Open Book Publishers titles, digital material and resources associated with this volume are available from our website:
http://www.openbookpublishers.com/product.php/78

ISBN Hardback: 978-1-906924-40-9
ISBN Paperback: 978-1-906924-39-3
ISBN Digital (pdf): 978-1-906924-41-6
ISBN ebook (epub): 978-1-906924-48-5
ISBN ebook (mobi): 978-1-906924-49-2

Index by Indexing Specialists (UK) Ltd
Cover image: *Identities* by Arthur Buxton

All paper used by Open Book Publishers is acid-free and SFI (Sustainable Forestry Initiative), and PEFC (Programme for the Endorsement of Forest Certification Schemes) Certified.

Printed in the United Kingdom and United States by
Lightning Source for Open Book Publishers

Contents

Additional Resources

In 2011/2012 the Commonwealth Secretariat is planning to take forward an extensive programme of action in the area of Civil Paths to Peace (CPP) including the following initiatives:

Pilot 'youth dialogue and action forums' in Commonwealth countries to facilitate discussions and actions on CPP issues in order to promote understanding, respect, tolerance and a culture of peaceful coexistence through dialogue and inclusive activities.

A resource pack on CPP. The proposed resource pack will have teaching and training modules on the CPP related topics such as respect and understanding, multiple identities, tolerance, conflict, violence and dialogue etc. It will be developed on a learner-centred-methodology where students and trainees will use games, role plays, stories, and exercises to learn and practice the CPP concepts and values by actually engaging in these activities.

Training programmes for Commonwealth journalists. A set of training programmes are proposed to be developed for the Commonwealth journalists and media personnel on CPP related topics such as 'responsible reporting of conflicts', ' skills for developing multiple narratives', 'promoting a culture of tolerance through media', and 'role of media in confidence building' etc.

A publication on CPP Good practices in the Commonwealth countries. The proposed book will showcase case studies where youth, women, education and media have played a positive role in preventing conflicts and promoting peace. This reference book will be used in CPP education and training programmes.

Further information about these developments, together with other digital resources related to the Civil Paths to Peace and this publication, will be available from the *Peace and Democratic Society* page on the Open Book Publishers website:

http://www.openbookpublishers.com/product.php/78

Part I

Violence and Civil Society[1]

Amartya Sen

1.

The widespread prevalence of terrorism and political violence in the contemporary world has led to many initiatives in recent years aimed at removing the scourge. Military ways for trying to secure peace have sometimes been rapidly deployed, with less informed justification in some cases than in others. And yet group violence through systematic instigation is not exclusively, nor primarily, a military challenge. It is fostered in our divisive world through capturing people's minds and loyalties, and through exploiting the varying allegiance of those who are wholly or partly persuaded. Some are 'inspired' – and prodded – into joining various movements for promoting violent actions against targeted groups, but a much larger number of influenced people do not take part in any violent activities themselves. They can nevertheless hugely contribute to generating a political climate in which the most peaceful of people come to tolerate the most egregious acts of intolerance and brutality, on some hazily perceived grounds of 'self-defence,' or 'just retaliation,' against the wrong-doing 'enemy.'

Amartya Sen would like to thank the Centre for History and Economics and, in particular, Inga Huld Markan and Neesha Harnam, for their research support. He would also like to thank Dr Corin Throsby, Senior Editor at Open Book Publishers.
1 This essay draws on my lecture at the University College London, on 2nd June 2009, on 'Violence in Society,' and also on my book *Identity and Violence: The Illusion of Destiny* (New York: Norton and London and Delhi: Penguin, 2006).

The Commonwealth Commission report called *Civil Paths to Peace*, which was published in 2007 and presented to the Heads of Commonwealth governments, focused particularly on the causes and ways of preventing terrorism and cultivated violence that has been in ascendancy for some years now and afflict or threaten the lives of nearly two billion people in the Commonwealth countries as well as the rest of the world.[2] The report does not dispute that military initiatives can sometimes be of limited use, when they are well informed, well executed, and adequately supplemented by well thought-out civilian measures. But when they are badly informed, or based on faulty reasoning, or inadequately linked to civil measures, they can not only fail to achieve their goals but in fact generate immensely counterproductive results, generating further hostilities. Civil initiatives, at the national as well as global level, are essential for successfully confronting organized violence and terrorism in the world today.

These civil paths are part of the engagement of democracy in the broad sense – that of 'government by discussion' – analysed by John Stuart Mill in particular. Democracy is more than a collection of specific institutions, such as balloting and elections – these institutions are important too, but as parts of a bigger engagement involving dialogue, freedom of information, and unrestricted discussion. These are also the central features of civil paths to peace.

The ways and means of pursuing these civil routes make a great many demands on us, but include, very importantly, the need for overcoming confused and flammable readings of the world.[3] While we human beings all have many affiliations – related to nationality, language, religion, profession, neighbourhood, social commitments and other connections – the cultivation of group violence proceeds through separating out exactly

---

2 *Civil Paths to Peace* (London: Commonwealth Secretariat, 2007). This is the Report of the Commonwealth Commission on Respect and Understanding re-published in this volume. The Commission included, in addition to me, John Alderdice, Kwame Anthony Appiah, Adrienne Clarkson, Noeleen Heyzer, Kamal Hossain, Elaine Sihoatani Howard, Wangari Muta Maathai, Ralston Nettleford, Joan Rwabyomere and Lucy Turnbull. I take this opportunity to express my deep appreciation of the wonderful work done by each of them. I am also grateful to the Commonwealth Secretariat for making this joint work possible.

3 On this and related issues, see Anthony Appiah, *The Ethics of Identity* (Princeton, NJ: Princeton University Press, 2005), and *Cosmopolitanism: Ethics in a World of Strangers* (New York: Norton, 2006); and Amartya Sen, *Identity and Violence: The Illusion of Destiny* (New York: Norton and London: Penguin, 2006).

one affiliation as our only significant identity. Even the gigantic violence of the First World War drew on singularly prioritizing the division of nationalities, ignoring the commonalities that could have united the Germans, the French and the British, rather than inducing them to kill each other. Right now, the divisiveness of a solitarist priority is increasingly based on the championing of religious identity, ignoring all other affiliations, and this gross understanding of humanity is much used by today's terrorists and other cultivators of group-based violence, who marry the classificatory singularity with aggressive readings of religious divisions. That confrontational outlook receives support, rather than resistance, from the increased popularity in the West of the supposedly unique significance of religious divisions, which is seen as dividing the world into allegedly disparate civilisations, characterized mainly by religion, and this is supplemented by some kind of inevitability of a clash between distinct 'civilisations.'

It is important to facilitate, rather than hinder, the understanding that human beings, with a variety of concerns and affiliations, need not be constantly at loggerheads with each other. If the institutional changes needed for pursuing civil paths to peace call for clarity of thought, they also demand, as the report discusses, organized policies, programmes and initiatives with the necessary versatility. Breadth of reach is crucial here. Indeed, even the well-meaning but excessively narrow approach of concentrating single-mindedly on expanding the dialogue between religious groups (much championed right now) can seriously undermine other civil engagements, linked with language, literature, cultural functions, social interactions and political commitments. And that can be a serious loss even from the point of view of peace and the overcoming of violence related to religious differences, since these other commitments and concerns help to resist the exploitation of religious differences which begins by downplaying – or dismissing – all other affiliations. The battle for people's minds cannot be won on the basis of a seriously incomplete understanding of the wealth of social differences that make individual human beings richly diverse in distinct ways. An exclusive focus on religious differences – not only for the purpose of fomenting disaffection but also for the 'amity of religions' – tends to characterize people simply in terms of their respective religions, thereby undermining all other affiliations that cut across religious boundaries. The diversity of civil society engagements needs support, not supplanting. For example, Bangladesh's success in burying religion-based violence as well as in curbing the hold of religious extremism has been helped greatly by focusing on linguistic identity and the richness of Bengali literature, music and culture, in addition to fostering secular politics, rather than holding inter-religious dialogues.

This does not, however, indicate that organized dialogue between different religious groups cannot ever serve any useful purpose. If such dialogues are arranged and understood as discussions on one selected aspect of the multiple identities of human beings, and if they are aimed specifically at eliminating some contemporary sources of tension without denying the unity that is fostered by a fuller recognition of the many different affiliations of human beings, then they can contingently be quite useful in reducing political tensions. This is indeed the approach that has been strongly advanced by Jorge Sampaio, the former President of Portugal who is now the 'United Nations High Representative of for the Alliance for Civilizations.' As Sampaio argues, 'cultural diversity has become a major political issue challenging modern democracies, pluralism, citizenship and social cohesion, as well as peace and stability among nations.'[4] It is right to pursue the institutional contribution that appropriately organized dialogues can make in addressing this political challenge. The important thing is to place the contrast of cultures and religions within a broader context of diverse diversities of human beings, which is what Sampaio has advocated. We differ from each other in many different ways, related to language, literature, profession, class, gender, residence and many others, in addition to religion, and while sometimes inter-group conversations on religious differences may help, at other times the differences even of religious backgrounds can be more easily tackled by focusing on other identities that challenge the cultivated prioritiaation of religious differences. There is room for both types of initiatives, but we have to be careful in making sure that in the process of fostering inter-religious amity we do not end up reducing human beings, explicitly or by implication, into one dimension only – in this case the religious dimension.

Cultivation of hostility can also be resisted by the working of the media, of political processes, of educational activities, and other means of generating mutual understanding. As the report discusses, while each

---

4 Jorge Sampaio, *The Road from Madrid to Istanbul and Beyond* (New York: Alliance of Civilizations, 2009), p. 13.

government can – and must – do a great deal more to help the spread of information and understanding, and the functioning of inclusive social activities, there is need also for widespread co-operation at the social and political level across the borders of each country.

Civil paths to peace include the removal, to the extent possible, of gross economic inequalities, social humiliations and political disenfranchisement, which can contribute to generating confrontation and hostility. Purely economic measures of inequality, such as the ratio of incomes of top and bottom groups, do not bring out the social dimension of the economic inequality involved. For example, when the people in the lowest income bracket have different non-economic characteristics in terms of race (such as being black rather than white), or immigration status (such as being recent arrivals rather than older residents), then the significance of the economic inequality is substantially magnified by its 'coupling' with other non-economic divisions.

Acts of terrorism and homicide are, of course, criminal activities calling for effective security measures, and no serious analysis of group violence can fail to take note of that basic understanding. But the analysis cannot end there, since many social, economic and political initiatives can be undertaken to confront and defeat the appeal on which the fomenters of violence and terrorism draw to get active foot soldiers and passive sympathisers. Central to the work of the Commission has been the Commonwealth's traditional approach of using multilateralism, making the best possible use of shared commitments, broad dialogues, and the willingness to discuss.

2.

The presence of violence and the fear of it have a huge impact on our lives, our well-being and our freedoms. And yet they are far less studied as social phenomena than many other subjects to which the social sciences have devoted much fuller attention. Questions of human security and its violation have been, to some extent, crowded out by the priority given to other – more expansionist – questions, such as economic growth of countries and regions, social and economic development of different parts of the world, and the demands of educational and cultural progress.

The good news, however, is that the subject of human security is receiving greater attention now than it had until rather recently. The reasons are not always comforting, in particular the increase of insecurities that plague human lives coming from group-based violence and the decline of the peaceful life of towns and human settlements. The need to pay some attention to conservation rather than just expansion is becoming increasingly clearer.

It may be useful to begin by briefly discussing the issues that have to be sorted out in order to have a clearer understanding of insecurity in general and of violence in particular. The Commonwealth Commission that produced the report *Civil Paths to Peace* focused particularly on causes and ways of preventing the spread of terrorism and cultivated violence that seem to be engulfing the world and which threaten, directly or indirectly, more than 1.8 billion people in Commonwealth countries. Our analyses and recommendations for action might be of some interest, we also hoped, for other parts of the world as well.

In the Commission we were bothered by the fact that the ways and means of dealing with threats of violence have increasingly gone in the direction of military, rather than civil, initiatives. Civil paths to peace have always been and still remain the basic way of successfully confronting violence and terrorism. The Commission concentrated on the ways and means of doing this.

A focus on action is ultimately what we need but there is a prior necessity of understanding why and how we face the adversities that we do face. We also have to separate out what we can clearly understand and what is not entirely clear as our intellectual engagement stands at present. We have to sit back a little and take our time when the problems we face are complex and ill-understood. As Buddha said more than 2,500 years ago, the solution to most problems lies ultimately in clearer understanding, and that demands intellectual engagement, and not merely prompt action.

3.

I begin with two contrasts involving the idea of human security: first, between human security and what is called 'national security', and second, between human security and the more established notion of 'human development'. The concept of national security can be defined in many different ways, and given the importance that the insignia of the term has acquired, there may well be much merit in trying to broaden appropriately the use of the expression 'national security.' But traditionally, national security, which is sometimes used synonymously with 'state security,' concentrates primarily on safeguarding what is perceived as national robustness, which has only an indirect connection with the security of human beings who live in these states. National security, in that aggregative and somewhat distanced form, has been studied over the centuries, and it is fortunate for us – people living in different countries in the world – that the demands of human security, which can go well beyond the concerns of national security (narrowly defined) are receiving more global attention today. Examination of the sources of insecurity of human lives, coming from violence, poverty, disease, and other widespread maladies, brings to light the far-reaching role of social, economic, political and cultural influences that the limited concept of national security cannot easily capture. The focus of security that interests people has to concentrate on the lives of the people, not the vigour of the state.

That contrast may be clear enough, but in delineating human security adequately, it is also important to understand how the idea of human security relates to – and differs from – other human-centred concepts, particularly that of human development. The idea of human development is not alienated from individual human lives in the way that some characterizations of national security can be, but human development too has its own specialized priorities, which need not be the same as the concerns of human security. It is, therefore, particularly important to ask what the idea of human security can add to these well-established ideas, particularly human development.

The human development approach, pioneered among others by the visionary economist Mahbub ul Haq (whom I was privileged to have as a close friend from our student days together at Cambridge to his untimely death in 1998), has done much to enrich and broaden the literature on development. I say with a declaration of interest and involvement, since I worked closely with Mahbub ul Haq, and among other things, helped him to devise the now much-used Human Development Index (HDI). I would claim that Mahbub's insights have deeply enlightened the understanding of development in general and development economics in particular in quite a decisive way. In particular, the human development approach has helped to shift the focus of developmental attention away from an overarching concentration on the growth of inanimate objects of convenience, such as commodities produced reflected in the gross domestic product or the gross national product), to the quality and richness of human lives, which depend on a great many influences, of which commodity production is only one.[5] Human development is concerned with removing the various hindrances that restrain and restrict human lives, and prevent its blossoming. Some of these concerns are indeed reflected in the HDI, which has served as something of a flagship of the human development approach, but the human development approach as a whole is much broader than what can be encapsulated into one numerical index of the HDI. The wide range and long reach of the human development perspective have motivated a vast literature, with increasing informational coverage of different aspects of human lives.

Why can't we, it can be asked, integrate our concern with human security and with violence in society within the broad coverage of the human development approach? Part of the reason is that, the more we put into one index or one approach, the less becomes the weights that can be placed on the other elements to which the index or the approach also caters. For example, the HDI is just one number, and if we want it take note of violence as well, then the relative focus on other factors already included – life expectancy, education, avoidance of economic penury – would to that extent weaken. We can certainly include the overcoming of violence and insecurity within the broad picture of human development, but if we want to do justice to each of the concerns that we include within one perspective, then we need to pay some special attention to each of them, rather than seeing each merely as a part of a very large whole.

There is another reason why we have to go beyond embedding our concern with violence and security within the broad vision of the human development approach, even though there is no conflict between these different concerns. The idea of human development has an especially buoyant quality, since it is concerned with progress and augmentation. It is, as it were, out to conquer fresh territory on behalf of enhancing human lives, and for that reason perhaps far too upbeat to focus on rearguard actions needed to secure features of our lives that have to be safeguarded. This is where the notion of human security becomes particularly relevant. Human security as an idea

---

5 See the very first *Human Development Report 1990* (New York: United Nations, UNDP, 1990), and the subsequent volumes. See also Sakiko Fukuda-Parr and Shiva Kumar, eds., *Readings in Human Development* (Oxford, New Delhi and New York: Oxford University Press, 2003).

provides a necessary supplement to the expansionist perspective of human development for it pays direct attention to what in the insurance literature is called 'downside risks.' The insecurities that threaten human survival or the safety of daily life, or expose human beings to the uncertainty of disease and pestilence, or subject vulnerable people to abrupt penury related to economic downturns (as we are experiencing today), demand that special attention be paid to the dangers of sudden deprivation. Human security demands protection from these dangers and also calls for the empowerment of people so that they can cope with and overcome – and when possible prevent – the incidence and reach of these hazards.

I am specifically concerned here with problems of violence in society, arising both from organized and unorganized mischief, but we have to examine the correlates of violence – its threats and the fears it generates – in the broader perspective of human security in general. There is a contrast there with both human development and national security: violence and other sources of human insecurity demand more systematic attention than they have so far tended to get.

4.

The question of violence engaged Nadine Gordimer and Kenzaburo Oe in a correspondence the two great writers had in 1998.[6] Gordimer noted that she 'should not have been surprised' that in writing to each other they were so 'preoccupied by the question of violence.' She went on to explain: 'This is a 'recognition' between two writers, but it goes further. It is the recognition of writers' inescapable need to read the signs society gives out cryptically and to try to make sense of what these really mean.' That need – indeed that *inescapable* need – to understand the question of violence not only influences writers like Gordimer and Oe, who illuminate us with their perceptive insights. It also makes all of us worry and fret and wonder, in trying to understand what we ourselves observe and what we can learn from reading others, and what we could possibly add of our own, if we only knew how.

The signs that 'society gives out cryptically,' to use Gordimer's discerning phrase, engage us all, in one way or another. Questions

---

6 Nadine Gordimer, *Living in Hope and History: Notes from the Century* (London: Bloomsbury, 1999), pp. 84-102.

of violence and insecurity are omnipresent in the world around us. If peace is in our dreams, war and violence are constantly in our eyes and ears. The terrible toll of human insecurity is recognized across the world.[7] What must, however, be avoided are ready-made answers that have a little plausibility (not no plausibility, but only very little), and which are then used to arrive at elaborate social policies, which neglect huge parts of the real connections.

On the grand subject of the root causes of contemporary global violence, theories abound – as theories are prone to. However, two particular lines of theorizing have come to receive much more attention than most others. One approach is primarily cultural and social, and often focuses on such concepts as identity, tradition and civilisation. The other is largely economic and political, and tends to focus on poverty, inequality and deprivation.

The main thesis I would like to present here is that the economic, social and cultural issues need serious efforts at integration. This exercise is spurned both by the crudely fatalistic theorists of civilisational clash and by the simple 'economistic' theorists who focus on poverty as the main cause of violence and, despite catching some part of the reality, may end up falling for the temptation to over-simplify the world which they wish to reform. I would argue that it is a mistake to look for ready-made reasons for remedying economic injustice so as to appeal even to those who are, for whatever reason, not revolted by injustice itself and yet hate – or are terrified of – the threat of violence.

Cultural theories tend to look at conflicts connected with modes of living as well as religious beliefs and social customs. That line of reasoning can lead to many different theories, some more sophisticated than others. It is perhaps remarkable that the particular cultural theory that has become the most popular in the world today is also perhaps also the crudest. This is the approach of seeing global violence as the result of something that is called 'the clash of civilizations.' The approach defines some postulated entities that are called 'civilisations'

---

7 A few years ago when I was privileged to chair, in the enlightening company of Dr. Sadako Ogata, the Commission for Human Security which reported to the U.N. Secretary General and the Prime Minister of Japan (the Japanese Government had taken the initiative in setting up this Commission), we were impressed to see how widely the interest in human security is shared across the world. See *Human Security Now. Commission on Human Security* (United Nations Publications: New York, 2003).

in primarily religious terms, and it goes on to contrast the 'Islamic world,' the 'Judeo-Christian Western world,' the 'Buddhist world,' the 'Hindu world,' and so on. It is the intrinsic hostility among civilisations that make them prone, it is argued in this high theory, to clash with each other.[8]

Underlying the approach of civilisational clash is an oddly artificial view of history, according to which these distinct civilisations have grown separately, like trees on different plots of land, with very little overlap and interaction. And today, as these disparate civilisations with their divergent histories face one another in the global world, they are firmly inclined, we are told, to clash with each other – a tale, indeed a gripping tale, of what can, I suppose, be called 'hate at first sight.' This make-believe account has little use for the actual history of huge historical interactions and constructive movements of ideas and influences across the borders of countries and regions in so many different fields – literature, arts, music, mathematics, science, engineering, trade, commerce, and other human engagements. The civilisational theorists are not entirely wrong in assuming that people are often suspicions of foreigners about whom they know little – possibly only about a few odd beliefs and practices that 'those foreigners' are supposed to have. However, more knowledge of each other can generate understanding rather than greater hostility. The civilisational theorists in this mode have tended to feed ignorant suspicion of 'the others' through their confident presumption that coming closer to each other as human beings must somehow aggravate those suspicions rather than helping to allay them.

Aside from missing out much of world history, the civilisational approach also takes a mind-boggling shortcut in trying to understand our sense of identity, with all it diversities and complexities, in terms of just a single sense of belonging, to wit, our alleged perception of oneness respectively with our so-called civilisation. It is through this huge oversimplification that the job of understanding diverse human beings of the world is metamorphosed, in this rugged approach to humanity, into looking at the different civilisations: personal differences are then seen as if they must be parasitic on civilisational contrasts.

---

8 This theory has received its definitive exposition in Samuel Huntington's widely read book, *The Clash of Civilizations and the Remaking of World Order* (New York: Simon and Schuster, 1996).

Violence between persons is then interpreted, in this approximate theory, as animosity between distinct civilisations, which is seen as a kind of all-powerful generic backdrop behind the frontage of human relations. Thus, in addition to its dependence on an imaginary history of the world, the civilisational explanation of global violence is largely moored on a particular 'solitarist' approach to human identity, which sees human beings as members of exactly one group defined by their native civilisation or religion.

A solitarist approach is, in fact, an excellent way of misunderstanding nearly everyone in the world. In our normal lives, we see ourselves as members of a variety of groups – we belong to all of them. The same person can be, without any contradiction, a South African citizen, of Asian origin, with Indian ancestry, a Christian, a socialist, a woman, a vegetarian, a jazz musician, a doctor, a feminist, a heterosexual, a believer in gay and lesbian rights, a jazz enthusiast, and one who believes that the most important problem that the world faces today is to make cricket more popular across the globe, breaking the spell of 'silly' games like baseball. Each of these identities can be of significance to the person, depending on the problem at hand and the context of choice, and the priorities between them could be influenced by one's own values as well as by social pressures. There is no reason to think that whatever civilisational identity a person has – religious, communal, regional, national or global – must invariably dominate over every other relation or affiliation a person may have.

Trying to understand global violence through the lens of the clash of civilizations does not bear much scrutiny, because the reasoning is so crude. But it must also be recognized that reductionist cultivations of singular identities have indeed been responsible for a good deal of what can be called 'engineered bloodshed' across the world. The engineering takes mostly the form of fomenting and cultivating alienated perceptions of differences. These conflicts are not just spontaneous unfoldings of a 'natural and inescapable' clash.

We may be suddenly informed by instigators that we are not just Yugoslavs but actually Serbs ('we absolutely don't like Albanians'), or that we are not just Rwandans or Kigalians or Africans, but specifically Hutus who must see Tutsis as enemies. I recollect from my own childhood in immediately pre-independent India, how the Hindu-Muslim riots suddenly erupted in the 1940s, linked with the politics of partition, and the speed with which the broad human beings of summer were suddenly transformed, through ruthless cultivation of communal alienation, into brutal Hindus and fierce Muslims of the winter. Hundreds of thousands perished at the hands of activists who, led by the designers of carnage, killed others on behalf of — for the *cause* of — those who are abruptly identified as their 'own people,' defined entirely by religion and religious community.

5.

Identity politics can certainly be mobilized very effectively in the cause of violence. And yet it can also be effectively resisted through a broader understanding of the richness of human identities. Our disparate associations may divide us in particular ways, and yet there are other identities, other affiliations, that defy any particular division. A Hutu who is recruited in the cause of chastising a Tutsi is also a Rwandan, and an African, possibly a Kigalian, and indubitably a human being – identities that the Tutsis also share. Socially and culturally anchored theories are not wrong in noting that people can be made to fight each other through incitement to violence across some divisive classification, but when that happens, we have to look for explanations of why and how the instigations occur, and how that one identity is made to look like the only one that matters. The process of such cultivated violence cannot really be seen simply as something like the unfolding of human destiny.[9]

In a marvellous essay in her book *Writing and Being*, Nadine Gordimer quotes Proust's remark: 'Do not be afraid to go too far, for the truth lies beyond.'[10] Gordimer is talking here about three great writers: Naguib Mahfouz, Chinua Achebe and Amos Oz, respectively from Egypt, Nigeria and Israel. These countries are not only very different, but are in some conflicted relation with each other. Gordimer notes that 'the oppositional links are there,' and yet, she goes on to point out, 'these three writers do not expound the obvious, divided by race, country and religion, they enter by their separate ways territory unknown, in a common pursuit that doesn't have to be acknowledged in any treaty.'

---

9 This issue is more fully examined in my book, *Identity and Violence: The Illusion of Destiny* (2006).
10 Nadine Gordimer, 'Zaabalawi: The Concealed Side,' in *Writing and Being* (Cambridge, MA: Harvard University Press, 1995), p. 43.

The battle against the bloody illusion of destiny calls for clarity. A clearer understanding comes not only from the visions of insightful writers, but also in more mundane ways from the thoughts of very ordinary people. It is that understanding that the instigators want to break down, and here the powerful voice of the more insightful can give us all a determination that we may not find it easy to sustain. When Mahatma Gandhi moved around, unarmed and completely unprotected, through the riot-torn districts during the violence of Indian partition, he was not only bringing new ideas to some. He was also helping to build greater determination of those whose own ideas matched, perhaps in a somewhat vague form, his own, but who did not have quite the courage and defiant confidence that Gandhi brought to them.

6.

Aside from the need to disestablish the claim that alleged clashes of civilisations, religions or communities must be natural processes, it is also important to appreciate that no matter how momentous the religious differences may appear to be in the context of some warfare today, there are other divisions that also have the potential for creating strife and carnage. The violence of solitarist identity can have a tremendously varying reach. Indeed, the obsession with religions and so-called civilisations (based primarily on religious differences) has been so strong in contemporary global politics that there is a strong tendency to forget how other lines of identity divisions have been exploited in the past – indeed not so long ago – to generate very different types of violence and war, causing millions of deaths.

For example, appeals to country and nationality played a rousing role in the immensely bloody war in Europe between 1914–1918, and a shared religious background of Christianity did nothing to stop the Germans, the British and the French from tearing each other apart. The identity that was championed then was that of nationalism, with the huge patriotic fervour it generated. Before the horrors of the First World War took the freshly recruited Wilfred Owen's life in the battlefield, he had the time to write his own protest about values that glorify violent combat in the cause of one's identity with one's nation and fatherland:

My friend, you will not tell with such high zest
To children ardent for some desperate glory,
The old lie: Dulce et Decorum est
Pro Patria Mori.

Horace's ringing endorsement of the honour of death for (or *allegedly* for) one's country could be seen as catering to the violence of nationalism, and it was this invocation against which Owen was emphatically protesting.

Europeans today may not easily appreciate Owen's profound sense of frustration and protest. In fact, the understanding that seemed well 'beyond' the 'too far' in Europe during the First World War, or for that matter during the Second, is now altogether customary and commonplace across Europe. The Germans, the French and the British mix with each other in peace and tranquillity and sit together to decide what to do in their continent without reaching for their gun.

A similar vulnerability is present in many other divisions of identities that may, at one level, be made to look like an unstoppable march of violence based on its unique claim of importance, but which, at another – broader – level may be nothing other than an artificially fostered avowal that can be disputed and displaced by a great many other solidarities and loyalties associated with different identities, including, of course, the broad commonality of our shared humanity.

7.

Let me, for the moment, leave the cultural approaches there. What about the other approach, the one of political economy? This line of reasoning sees poverty and inequality as the root causes of violence. It is not hard to see that the injustice of inequality can generate intolerance and that the suffering of poverty can provoke anger and fury. There is clearly much plausibility in seeing a connection between violence and poverty. For example, many countries have experienced – and continue to experience – the simultaneous presence of economic destitution and political strife. From Afghanistan and Sudan to Somalia and Haiti, there are plenty of examples of the dual adversities of deprivation and violence faced by people in different parts of the world. Given that co-existence, it is not at all unnatural to ask whether poverty kills twice – first through *economic privation*, and second through *political carnage*.

Poverty can certainly make a person outraged and desperate, and a sense of injustice can be a good ground for rebellion – even bloody rebellion. Furthermore, it is not uncommon to presume that a basic characteristic of an enlightened attitude to war and peace must be to go beyond the obvious and immediate causal features that can be plainly seen in a conflict, and must seek 'deeper' causes in social deprivation. In looking for such underlying causes, the economics of deprivation and inequity has a very plausible claim to attention. The belief that the root of discontent and disorder has to be sought in economic destitution has been fairly widely favoured by social analysts, in their attempt to look beyond the apparent and the obvious.

The straightforward thesis linking poverty with violence also has another appeal: that it looks ready for good use in the humane advocacy of concerted public action to end poverty. Those trying to eradicate poverty in the world are, naturally enough, tempted to invoke the apparent causal connection that ties violence to poverty, to seek the support of even those who are not moved by poverty itself. There has, in fact, been an increasing tendency in recent years to argue in favour of policies of poverty removal on the ground that this is the surest way to prevent political strife and turmoil. Basing public policy – international as well as domestic – on such an understanding has some evident attractions. It provides a politically powerful argument for allocating more public resources and efforts on poverty removal because of its presumed political rewards, taking us much beyond the direct moral case for doing this.

Since widespread physical violence seems to be more loathed and feared, especially by well-placed people, than the social inequity and deprivation – even extreme deprivation – of others, it is indeed tempting to be able to tell all, including the well-heeled, that terrible poverty will generate terrifying violence. Given the visibility and public anxiety about wars and disorders, the indirect justification of poverty removal – not for its own sake but for pursuing peace and quiet – has become, in recent years, a dominant part of the rhetoric of fighting poverty.

There is certainly a connection there, but is it really plausible to seek explanations of violence in a one-factor analysis of poverty and privation? While the temptation to go in this direction is easy to appreciate, the difficulty here lies in the possibility that if the causal connection proves to be not quite robust, then economic reductionism would not only have impaired our understanding of the world, but would also tend to undermine the declared rationale of the public commitment to remove poverty. This is a particularly serious concern, since poverty and massive inequality are terrible enough in themselves to provide ample reason for working for their removal – even if they did not have any further ill effects through indirect links. Just as virtue is its own reward, poverty is at least its own punishment. To look for some ulterior reason for fighting poverty through its effects on violence and conflict may make the argument apparently broader with a larger reach, but it can also make the reasoning much more fragile.

To see this danger is not the same as denying that poverty and inequality can – and do – have far-reaching connections with conflict and strife, but these connections have to be investigated and assessed with appropriate care and empirical strongmindedness. The temptation to summon economic reductionism may be sometimes effective in helping what we may see as a right cause (and may even have the arguably agreeable feature of catering to our frailty in giving us satisfaction from frightening the ethically obtuse by threatening them with the danger of bloody violence), but it is basically an unsound way to proceed and can indeed be seriously counterproductive for political ethics.

8.

The simple thesis linking poverty with violence is not only compromised by doubtful ethical use, it is also, as it happens, riddled with epistemic problems. The claim that poverty is responsible for group violence is empirically much too crude both because the linkage of poverty and violence is far from universally observed, and because there are other social factors that are also associated with poverty and violence.

When I gave the Lewis Mumford Lecture at the City College of New York in 2007, entitled 'The Urbanity of Calcutta,' I had the opportunity to comment on the remarkable fact that Calcutta (or Kolkata as we are now encouraged to spell the name in English in search of a closer correspondence with Bengali diction) is not only one of poorest cities in India – and indeed in the world – it so happens that it also has a very low crime rate. Indeed, in serious crimes, the poor city of Calcutta has the lowest incidence among all the Indian cities. The average incidence of murder in the 35 cities of India is 2.7 per 100,000 people – 2.9 for Delhi. The rate is 0.3 in Kolkata.[11] The same lowness of violent crime can be seen in looking at the total number of all violations of the Indian Penal Code put together. It also applies to crime against women, the incidence of which is very substantially lower in Calcutta than in all other major cities in India.

It also emerges that Indian cities in general are strikingly low in the incidence of violent crime by world standards, and Calcutta seems to have the lowest homicide rate not only in India, but also in the world. In 2005, Paris had a homicide rate of 2.3, London of 2.4, New York of 5.0, Buenos Aires of 6.4, Los Angeles 8.8, Mexico City of 17.0, Johannesburg 21.5, Sao Paulo 24.0, and Rio de Janeiro an astonishing 34.9.[12] Even the famously low-crime Japanese cities have more than three times the homicide rate of Calcutta, with 1.0 per 100,000 for Tokyo and 1.8 for Osaka, and only Hong Kong and Singapore come close to Calcutta (though still more than 60 per cent higher), at 0.5 per 100,000 each, compared with Calcutta's 0.3.

If all this appears to us to be an unfathomable conundrum, given Calcutta's poverty, that may be a reflection of the limitation of our thought, rather than a paradox of nature. Calcutta does, of course, have a long distance to go to eradicate poverty and to put its material house in order. It is important to remember that the low crime rate does not make those nasty problems go away. And yet there is something important to note – and even to celebrate – in the recognition that poverty does not inescapably produce violence, independently of political movements as well as social and cultural interactions.

Explanation of crime is not an easy subject for empirical generalizations, and even though there have been some attempts recently to understand the nature and incidence of crime in terms of the characteristics of the respective neighbourhoods, it is quite clear that there is still a long way to go for a fuller understanding of the picture.[13]

---

11 These figures are based on the data presented by the National Crime Record Bureau of India, *Crime in India 2005* (New Delhi: Government of India, 2007).

12 The data on the incidence of homicide in different cities have been collected from the respective municipal and national publications, and I am very grateful to Pedro Ramos Pinto for wonderful research assistance in this and related work.

13 See, for example, the illuminating collections of essays in Per-Olof H. Wilkstrom, and Robert J. Sampson, eds., *The Explanation of Crime: Context, Mechanisms and Development* (Cambridge: Cambridge University Press, 2006).

In my Mumford Lecture, I have tried to argue that Calcutta has benefited, among other causal factors, from the fact that it has had a long history of being a thoroughly mixed city, where neighbourhoods have not had the feature of sharp ethnic separation that some cities – in India as well as elsewhere – have. There are also many other social and cultural features that are undoubtedly relevant in understanding the relation between poverty and crime. For example, in trying to understand the high rates of violent crime in South Africa, it would be hard to overlook the connection with the legacy of apartheid. The linkage involves not only the inheritance of racial confrontation, but also the terrible effects of separated neighbourhoods and families that were split up for the economic arrangements that went with the philosophy of apartheid. But it would not be easy to explain why the belated attempts to generate mixed communities have also had the immediate effect of fostering crime committed *within* the newly mixed neighbourhoods in South Africa. Perhaps the legacy of a long history can only be wiped out rather slowly.

I am afraid we do not know enough about the empirical relations to be confident of what the exact causal connections here are, and I am acutely aware that there is need for humility here that social sciences invariably invite and frequently do not get. It does, however, seem fairly clear that the tendency to see a universal and immediate link between poverty and violence would be very hard to sustain. There is certainly a more complex picture that lies beyond the alleged straightforwardness of the poverty-violence relationship.

More specifically, if we look, in particular, at violence related to religion, ethnicity and community (the direction to which we are dispatched by many cultural theorists), the role of conscious politics as a barrier also demands a fuller recognition. For example, the prevailing politics of Calcutta and of West Bengal, which is very substantially left of centre, has tended to concentrate on deprivation related to class and, more recently, to uses and abuses of political power. That political focus, which is very distinct from religion and religion-based community, has made it much harder to exploit religious differences for instigating riots against minorities, as has happened, with much brutality, in some Indian cities, for example Bombay (or Mumbai) and Ahmedabad. Calcutta did have its full share of Hindu-Muslim riots related to the partition of India, which were rampant across the subcontinent. But over many decades later, there have been no such riots in this large city, unlike in many other urban conglomerates in India. Indeed, the whole sectarian agenda of cultivating communal divisiveness seems to have got substantially overturned by new political and social priorities that dominate the city.

And in this political development, the focus on economic poverty and inequality seems to have played, if anything, a constructive role in bringing out the ultimate triviality of religious differences in preventing social harmony. In the recognition of plural human identities, the increased concentration on class and other sources of economic disparity has made it very hard to excite communal passions and violence in Calcutta along the lines of a religious divide – a previously cultivated device that has increasingly looked strangely primitive and raw. The minorities, mainly Muslims and Sikhs, have had a sense of security in Calcutta that they have not always been able to enjoy in Bombay or Ahmedabad or Delhi.

If identities related to left-wing politics and class have had the effect of vastly weakening violence based on religious divisions and community contrasts in the Indian part of Bengal, a similar constructive influence can be seen on the other side of the border, in Bangladesh, coming from the power of identities of language, literature and music, which do not divide Muslims and Hindus into different – and exploitably hostile – camps. The more general point here is that an understanding of multiplicity of our identities can be a huge force in combating the instigation of violence based on a singular identity – particularly religious identity which is the dominant form of cultivated singularity in our disturbed world today.

9.

The economic connections between poverty and violence are quite complex and can hardly be captured by the simplicity of economic reductionism. For example, the violent history of Afghanistan cannot be unrelated to the poverty and indigence that the population have experienced, and yet to reduce the causation of violence there entirely to this singular economic observation would be to miss out the role of the Taliban and the politics of religious sectarianism and extremism. It would also leave out the part played by the history of Western military support – and incitement – to strengthen religious extremists in Afghanistan against the Russians, at a time when the Western leaders saw the Soviet Union to be something like a single-handed 'axis of evil.' And, at the same time, to dissociate the rise of fundamentalism and sectarian violence from all economic connections would also be a mistake. We must try to understand the different interconnections that work together, and often kill together. We need some investigative sophistication to understand what part is played by the economic components in the larger structure of an interactive social framework.

The empirical connections between poverty and violence are clearly significantly contingent on many other circumstances. There is, of course, no dearth of evidence of conflicts and confrontations in economies with a good deal of poverty and much inequality. But, at the same time, there are also other economies with no less poverty or inequality that seem to stay deeply and inertly sunk just in economic hardship, without generating serious political turbulence. Poverty can co-exist with peace and apparent tranquillity, and the causal reasoning linking poverty to violence has gaps that need to be acknowledged. Impoverishment can, of course, yield provocation to defy the established laws and rules, but it need not give people the initiative, courage and actual ability to do anything particularly violent.

Indeed, destitution can be accompanied not only by economic debility, but also by political impotence and debility. The emaciated victims of deprivation can be too frail and too dejected to fight and battle, and even to protest and holler. It is not surprising that intense suffering and inequity has often been accompanied by astonishing peace and deafening silence. For example, the famine years in the 1840s in Ireland were among the most peaceful, and there was little attempt by the hungry masses to intervene even as ship after ship sailed down the river Shannon laden with food, carrying it away from starving Ireland to well-fed England, by the pull of market forces (the English had more money to buy meat, poultry, butter and food items than the blighted Irish had). As it happens, the Irish do not have an exceptional reputation for excessive docility, and yet the famine years were, by and large, years of order and peace. London not only got away with extreme misgovernance of Ireland, they did not even have to face the violence of Irish mobs (even though the Irish famines had the largest share of mortality in total population among all the famines for which data exist). As Calgacus, the rebellious Scottish chief, said about Roman dominance of first century Britain: 'They make a wilderness and they call it peace.'

This does not, however, indicate that the poverty, starvation and inequity of the Irish famines had no long-run effects on violence in Ireland. Indeed, the memory of injustice and neglect had the effect of severely alienating the Irish from Britain, and contributed greatly to the violence that characterized Anglo-Irish relations over more than a century and a half. Economic destitution may not lead to an immediate rebellion, but it would be wrong to presume from this that there is no connection between poverty and violence. There is an important need here to look at connections over time – often a very long time – and also at the way the grievances of deprivation and maltreatment get merged with other factors, including, in the Irish case, a championing of national identity that seeks distancing from the English. The offensive nature of English caricatures of the Irish, going back all the way to Spenser's *Faerie Queene* in the sixteenth century, would be strongly reinforced by the experience of the famines of the 1840s under British rule, generating deep resentment against Ireland's more powerful neighbours who did so little to stop the starvation, and in many ways, even helped to aggravate it.

There is a similarity here with the experience of the Middle East. There are, of course, many influences that have made the situation as difficult there as it has been in recent decades, including the apparent difficulty of some world leaders to think clearly on the subject. But among the many connections, it is hard to ignore the memory of ill-treatment of the Middle East by Western powers during the colonial days, when the new masters could subdue one nation after another and draw — and redraw — the boundaries between countries just as they liked. That abuse of power did not cause many riots right then in the nineteenth century, but that silence of the vanquished — the peace of the trampled — does not indicate that the subject matter was gone forever, and would not leave behind a terrible memory of ill-treatment. As Flora Goforth remarked in Tennessee William's *The Milk Train Does Not Stop Here Anymore*, 'Life is all memory except for the one present moment that goes by you so quick you hardly catch it going.' Similarly, the new episodes of trampling and pulverization today — in Iraq and Palestine and elsewhere — will not be easily forgotten, I fear, for a long time in the future.

Despite the burden of history, there is a huge opportunity right now for the world to play a positive part in sustaining the powerful popular movements for democracy that have rapidly become a new reality of the Middle East over the last few months (even as I write this Introduction). The strong desire for democracy in the Arab world, which I discussed in my book *Identity and Violence* (2006), seems to have fought through the authoritarian barriers in most courageous ways, and there is a lot to be done right now to provide global support to this highly promising development in one of the most problematic regions in the world. Civil paths to peace across the world can both help and benefit from the powerful social initiatives that have challenged the tyranny and military might of entrenched regimes through essentially peaceful means, in favour of democracy and long-postponed 'governance by discussion' (to return to Mill's championing of that foundational idea of democracy).[14]

10.

If the strong but less immediate linking of poverty and injustice to violence has some weak plausibility (as I believe it does), then we have to see how the ideas of identity and culture add to the reach of these issues of political economy, rather than competing with their influence in an 'either this or that' way. The categories around which the provoked violence may proceed would have cultural and social distinctions of their own (linked with ethnicity or nationality or social background), but the possibility of instigating anger can be dramatically increased and magnified by historical association with economic and political inequity. Indeed, even the brutality of the Hutu activists against Tutsis made effective use of the fact that Tutsis had more of a privileged position in Rwanda than the Hutus typically had — this would have done nothing to justify what happened but the existence of that empirical connection is part of the study of violence of which we have to take notice. Poverty and inequality must have a role in promoting and sustaining violence, but that role, I would argue, has to be sought not through an exclusive concentration on deprivation and destitution in isolation from society and culture, but through looking for a larger and much more extensive framework with interactive roles of poverty and other features of society.

Similarly, while the fierce nastiness of Al Qaeda against Western

14 On this see my *The Idea of Justice* (London: Penguin and Cambridge, MA: Harvard University Press, 2009), Chapters 15-18.

targets cannot be justified by any invoking of history, the fact that those on whose name the terrorists work have had unequal treatment in the past from Western colonialists makes the invitation to barbarity that much easier to sell. The absence of an ethical justification of such a linkage does not eliminate the fact that it can nevertheless have much power in moving people to blind rage. Indeed, the tolerance of terrorism by an otherwise peaceful population is another peculiar phenomenon in many parts of the contemporary world, particularly those that feel they were badly treated in the past.

Inequalities of military strength, political power and economy might leave behind huge inheritances of discontent. This is so even when the process is not apparently linked with force and strong-armed behaviour, for example, the injustice of leaving hundreds of millions behind in global economic and social progress, or condemning millions of others to untreated medical maladies for ailments that can be eliminated or effectively controlled, but where the global economic mechanism fails to provide life-saving drugs to those who need them most.

11.

Economic, social and cultural issues need serious efforts at integration — an exercize that is spurned both by the fatalistic theorists of civilisational clash and by the hurried advocates of economic reductionism. Cultural and social factors as well as features of political economy are all important in understanding violence in the world today. But they do not work in isolation from each other, and we have to resist the tempting shortcuts that claim to deliver insight through their single-minded concentration on one factor or another, ignoring other important features of an integrated picture. Perhaps most importantly, we have reason to understand that these distinct causal antecedents of violence are not immovable objects that can defy and overwhelm all human efforts to create a more tolerable social order. These connections are more fully explored in the report of the Commonwealth Commission, *Civil Paths to Peace*, to which this essay is merely the introduction.

It is indeed important to see the often-neglected connection between clarity of understanding and the way society functions and operates. Indeed, but for the political vision that inspired South Africa's anti-apartheid movement, led by Nelson Mandela and also Desmond

Tutu, South Africa today would be covered not with reconciliation but with violent revenge against what had been one of the most cruel segregationist orders in the world. Similarly, the barbarity of world wars in the early twentieth century paved the way for the kind of social analyses which led, among other things, to the European Movement that would ultimately lead to the submerging of those national conflicts within Europe in the latter half of the century. The outcome that is entirely mundane now would have been very hard to imagine in the trenches and battlefields in the dark days of 1914 to 1918. Similarly, the huge expression of public demand for democracy that is unfolding in one country after another in the Middle East (Tunisia, Egypt, Libya and others) can be the beginning of the operation of a very different identity – different from religious prioritization as well as submission to authoritarianism – that would, unless suppressed by organized power of state governments or of religious extremism, bring about a major change in the politics of the Middle East.

It is not difficult to see that divisions can be exploited to generate violence, sometimes made more intense and fierce through the coupling of economic and social inequality with ethnic and cultural differences. Nor is it really surprising that those divisive lines of thinking can be overcome given some clarity of vision and understanding. What, however, is altogether magnificent is that what seems to lie far beyond feasibility today may become, through our own efforts, entirely achievable and thoroughly ordinary tomorrow. We can get strength from Proust and Gordimer: 'Do not be afraid to go too far, for the truth lies beyond.' That recognition, which is important in general, may be especially so in our moments of dejection about human insecurity in our trouble-ridden world.

Part II

Civil Paths to Peace

Report of the Commonwealth Commission on Respect and Understanding

Amartya Sen (Chairperson)
John Alderdice
Kwame Anthony Appiah
Adrienne Clarkson
Noeleen Heyzer
Kamal Hossain
Elaine Sihoatani Howard
Wangari Muta Maathai
Ralston Nettleford
Joan Rwabyomere
Lucy Turnbull

Members of the Commonwealth Commission on Respect and Understanding

Rt Hon. Lord John Alderdice (United Kingdom)
John, Lord Alderdice (United Kingdom) was from 1987 to 1998 leader of Northern Ireland's cross-community Alliance Party, and played a key role in the negotiation of the 1998 Belfast Agreement. He was the first Speaker of the new Northern Ireland Assembly from 1998 until 2004, and was then appointed as one of four international monitoring commissioners overseeing security normalization in Ireland. He sits on the Liberal Democrat benches in the House of Lords, and since 2005 has been the elected President of Liberal International - the world-wide federation of liberal political parties. He runs the Centre for Psychotherapy in Belfast and is a Visiting Professor in Psychiatry and Joint Chairman of the Critical Incident Analysis Group at the University of Virginia, with a special interest in the psychology of terrorism and violent political conflict.

Professor Kwame Anthony Appiah (Ghana) is Laurence S. Rockefeller University Professor of Philosophy and the University Center for Human Values at Princeton University. He has published widely in African and African-American literary and cultural studies, and in 1992, Oxford University Press published In My Father's House, which deals, in part, with the role of African and African-American intellectuals in shaping contemporary African cultural life. His most recent publications include *The Ethics of Identity* (2004) and *Cosmopolitanism: Ethics in a World of Strangers* (2006).

Rt Hon. Adrienne Clarkson (Canada) is an accomplished journalist and until 2005 she served as the 26th Governor General of Canada: she was the first Chinese Canadian and second woman to hold this position. She was also the first (and thus far only) Governor General to be awarded the Order of Canada prior to taking office. Clarkson is well known for her work in broadcasting, having hosted and produced several shows for the CBC between 1964 and 1982.

Dr Noeleen Heyzer (Singapore) is the first executive director from the South to head the United Nations Development Fund for Women (UNIFEM), the leading operational agency within the United Nations to promote women's empowerment and gender equality. She played a critical role in the Security Council's adoption of Resolution 1325 on Women, Peace and Security. Previously a policy adviser to Asian governments, in 1994–95 she played a key role in the preparatory process for the Fourth World Conference on Women in Beijing, including organizing 1,000 NGOs in the Asia Pacific region to develop the first ever NGO Action Plan. Dr Heyzer has been a founding member of numerous regional and international women's networks and has received several awards for leadership including the Dag Hammarskjöld medal in 2004.

Dr Kamal Hossain (Bangladesh) is a former Minister of Law and former Minister of Foreign Affairs of Bangladesh and is credited with being one of the principal authors of his country's National Constitution. Co-patron (and formerly Chair), of the Commonwealth Human Rights Initiative, and formerly UN Special Rapporteur on Human Rights in Afghanistan, he has recently been highlighting the plight of Afghan refugees and the need for international aid.

Ms Elaine Sihoatani Howard (Tonga) is the Executive Director of Tonga National Youth Congress (Nuku'alofa, Tonga), and Chairperson of the Commonwealth Youth Programme – South Pacific Regional Youth Caucus (RYC) (Honiara, Solomon Islands). She was awarded: Winner – Best Original Research Presentation at International Development Conference of New Zealand 2004, and Overall University Winner, University of Auckland Postgraduate Research Exposition 2004.

Professor Wangari Muta Maathai (Kenya) is the first African woman to win the Nobel Peace Prize (in 2004). An academic, Professor Maathai's role as an environmental campaigner began in 1977 when she formed an organization – primarily of women – known as the Green Belt Movement

– which mobilized poor women to plant some 30 million trees across Africa. Having been elected to parliament with an overwhelming 98 per cent of the vote in 2002, Professor Wangari Maathai was subsequently appointed by the president as Assistant Minister for Environment, Natural Resources and Wildlife in Kenya's ninth parliament.

The Honourable Ralston Milton Nettleford OM (Jamaica) better known as Rex Nettleford, is a Jamaican scholar, social critic and choreographer. A former Rhodes Scholar he is currently a Vice Chancellor Emeritus of the University of the West Indies where he pursued a first degree in History before proceeding to postgraduate studies at Oxford as a Rhodes Scholar. As a creative artist he founded in 1962 the National Dance Theatre Company of Jamaica, which under his direction has done much to incorporate traditional Jamaican/Caribbean music and movement into a formal balletic repertoire. He is the author of several books including *Mirror Mirror: Identity Race and Protest in Jamaica* and in 1971 compiled, edited, annotated and introduced the speeches and writings of Norman Manley in *Manley and the New Jamaica*. Nettleford established himself as a serious public historian and social critic and was awarded the Order of Merit by the State in recognition of his cultural and scholarly achievements. He was later appointed an ambassador-at-large by his native Jamaica.

HE Mrs Joan Rwabyomere (Uganda) is High Commissioner of Uganda to the UK and Ireland. As a qualified lawyer, she has worked extensively in both business and government. Her positions have included being Vice-Chairman of the Board of Directors, National Enterprises Corporation (1999–2000); Deputy-Director General, External Security (1996–1998); Minister of State for Agriculture (1995–1996); Director, Uganda Electricity Board (1989–1995); Chairman, Board of Directors, Uganda Civil Aviation Authority (1989–1995); Delegate to the EU–ACP Joint Assembly (1989–1995); and a Member of Parliament (1989–1996). Mrs Rwabyomere took up the position of High Commissioner to the UK having been High Commissioner of Uganda to Nigeria from 2001–2005. She has four children.

Mrs Lucy Turnbull (Australia) is an Australian businesswoman and former Lord Mayor of Sydney. For many years she worked as a commercial lawyer and in investment banking. She is a member of the board of the Redfern Waterloo Authority, which was established in 2005 to assist the NSW government to develop a comprehensive plan (social and spatial) for the Redfern–Waterloo area of Sydney, one of the most socio-economically disadvantaged suburbs in Australia. From 1999–2004 she was a member of the Central Sydney Planning Committee. She chairs the Salvation Army Red Shield Appeal in Sydney, and is a member of the Board of Governors of the Woolcock Institute of Medical Research, a respiratory and sleep research institute. She is a board member of Melbourne IT Limited, a publicly listed internet services company, and is a board member of several other private companies in the technology and financial services industries.

Other participants at the meetings:

Professor Shamit Saggar, Professor of Political Science, University of Sussex, and Visiting Professor, University of Toronto

Dr Sarah Ladbury, freelance social development consultant

Commonwealth Secretariat:

Rt Hon Donald McKinnon, Secretary-General

Mrs Florence Mugasha, Deputy Secretary-General

Mr Amitav Banerji, Director, Secretary-General's Office

Mr Matthew Neuhaus, Director, Political Affairs Division

Ms Alexandra Jones, Director, Strategic Planning and Evaluation Division

Ms Daisy Cooper, Planning Officer, Strategic Planning and Evaluation Division

Ms Sabhita Raju, Political Affairs Officer, Good Offices, Political Affairs Division

The Commission is indebted to Shamit Saggar and Sarah Ladbury for their background papers which greatly assisted their discussions.

Executive Summary

This report, which contains the analyses and findings of the Commonwealth Commission on Respect and Understanding, has been guided by the need to develop policy recommendations for Commonwealth Heads of Government, informed by a clear appreciation of the importance and reach of the underlying concepts that give the Commission its name. This report is, thus, both about recommendations of policies to be pursued and about the ways in which policy thinking has to adapt to the realities of the world in which we live. If the cultivation of respect and understanding is both important in itself and consequential in reducing violence and terrorism in the world, the link between the two lies in the understanding that cultivated violence is generated through fomenting disrespect and fostering confrontational misunderstandings. While the report discusses various policy directions as well as particular policy measures, the Commission has requested the Secretary-General to follow up with further specifications for an action programme in consultation with the respective governments.

The Commission was established in response to the decision at the 2005 Commonwealth Heads of Government Meeting (CHOGM) to request the Commonwealth Secretary-General 'to explore initiatives to promote mutual understanding and respect among all faiths and communities in the Commonwealth'. The Commission, appointed by the Secretary-General and comprising eleven experts from a wide range of disciplines and professional backgrounds, met twice in 2006–07 to prepare its report, and also had extensive correspondence and interchange of ideas and suggestions.

With a third of the world's population, the Commonwealth is home to rich and poor, young and old, and people of every colour and creed. It is also an organization that strives hard to make democracy a way of life. Its composition is inclusive of all political and economic groupings – its 53 members[1] come from every geographical region, represent every stage of development, and include people from all the major religions.

The shared history and traditions of Commonwealth members has yielded administrative, educational and legal lessons that provide fertile ground for the exchange of ideas and best practice. The Commonwealth has used these to good effect, particularly in its support for the poorest and the most marginalized – women, young people, indigenous groups, and the rural poor – particularly those in least-developed countries, including those in small island states.

The Commission believes that the response to confrontational problems should be rooted in the Commonwealth's agreed fundamental emphasis on human rights, liberties, democratic societies, gender equality, the rule of law and a political culture that promotes transparency, accountability and economic development. It is also important to appreciate that the Commonwealth is not just a family of nations; it is also a family of peoples. Furthermore, the Commonwealth provides a shared forum in which governments and civil society meet as partners and as equals. With over 85 pan-Commonwealth professional associations and civil society organizations, the Commonwealth family connects through institutional as well as personal links, and operates through cultural as well as political, social and economic affiliations.

Drawing on the participation of and consultation with its civil society partners, the Commonwealth makes decisions on the basis of negotiation, dialogue, precedent and consensus. This so-called 'Commonwealth approach' of working ensures that members respect each other and try to understand, as fully as possible, the points of view of others. It is to this that the great leader of our time – and former President of South Africa – Nelson Mandela referred in 1994 when he argued that 'the Commonwealth makes the world safe for diversity'.

---

1 There are now 54 member countries: Rwanda joined the Commonwealth in 2009.

The need for new thinking about the conflicts in the world

Cultural – indeed 'civilisational' – explanations of world conflict have acquired much popularity recently, to some extent inspired by Samuel Huntington's thesis on the inevitability of 'the clash of civilisations'. That thesis has gained further popularity since the terrible events of 9/11. There has been much discussion about what appears to be an irreconcilable divide between the values of 'us' and 'them' – most notably between the 'West and the rest', between Muslims and non-Muslims. While many have argued, both before and after 9/11, that culture is neither the defining nor the only fault line over which people conflict, the question of how to address the many root causes of conflict has gained a new urgency.

This report has particularly focused on the issues of terrorism, extremism, conflict and violence, for they are much in ascendancy in the contemporary world and afflict the Commonwealth countries as well as the rest of the world. The report investigates the different ways in which such conflicts and violence emerge and are sustained and enlarged. While the cultural influences are among the forces that can contribute to disrespect, misunderstanding and violence, they are not the only causal factors, nor are they immutable or irresistible. Indeed, much can be done to prevent the violence that may be thrust on us by promoters of belligerent agendas. For this we need a departure from old ways of thinking about the centrality and the alleged inviolability of cultural confrontations.

The focus can be put instead on understanding the mechanisms through which violence is cultivated through advocacy and recruitment, and on the pre-existing inequalities, deprivations and humiliations on which those advocacies draw. These diagnoses also clear the way for methods of countering fostered disaffection and violence. In various chapters the different connections are explored and examined to yield general policy recommendations.

Inequality, grievance and history

Beginning with the connection between respect and understanding, on the one hand, and disquiet, disaffection and violence, on the other (Chapter 1), the report explores the various ways through which violence is generated and sometimes wilfully nurtured (Chapter 2).

The role of poverty and inequality in fostering disquiet and hatred, and violence in particular, call for some sophistication of analysis, since the connections are not by any means mechanical and invariant. And yet there are connections, which are discussed in the report (Chapter 3). In addition to manifest inequality, the psychological dimensions of humiliation also demand some depth of analysis.

The history of the world matters to contemporary problems, since the effects of past maltreatment and humiliation can last for a very long time (Chapter 4). The civil paths must, therefore, include addressing past as well as present humiliations. The connections over time, for example through colonial history, are important to understand to appreciate the roots of the actual continuation of inequality and the perceptions of injustice that are seen as being meted out to less privileged parts of humanity. Sometimes the sources of a sense of iniquity and humiliation are real, and they call for remedying (the Scarman Report chaired by Lord Scarman in 1982 is cited here as a good example of policy recommendations following from visionary but detailed diagnoses). When, as is sometimes the case, the confrontational perceptions are exaggerated by confusion (or magnified through extremist instigation), those misapprehensions should still have to be addressed through civil means, with good use of discussion, open scrutiny and a willingness on the part of others to listen to complaints and grievances. The outcomes of these changes would have to be periodically evaluated, in a systematic way, since complex and long-standing problems are not easily eradicated.

Participation, the media and education

If participation is an important part of a suitably multilateral approach to world peace (following the so-called Commonwealth approach), the critical role of political participation within the borders of a country can hardly be over-emphasized (Chapter 5). Attention has to be paid to the reach of the forums for discussion, from central to local, and to ensure that deprived persons are not excluded from the opportunity of joining in and voicing their questions and concerns.

Even though some champions of what they call 'multiculturalism' have shown great hostility to the idea of a national identity, there is nothing in that political concept that reduces the relevance of culture, or religion, or language, in their own respective domains. Indeed, a national identity can be used to give each person an acknowledged equality in political participation, irrespective of religion, race, caste, dialect, or community, or – for that matter – their date of immigration (when that is an issue).

The development of civil society is another area to which special attention has to be paid. A variety of groupings, based on different affiliations, need encouragement and support: the diversity of associations helps to bring neglected concerns to public attention. Governments and civil society organizations have to ensure that those who are consulted are representative of widely held sentiments that can be fairly attributed to the respective groups. Vocal but peaceful political participation can then have the dual role of (1) leading to a more informed making of public policy, and (2) removing discontent about not being heard, which can ultimately contribute to rage and violence.

The Commission believes it is particularly important to pay special attention to women's political participation, since this is often seriously neglected. In this field, the Commonwealth has quite a wealth of initiatives and experiences (some of which the report has discussed), and the different countries can benefit from the experiences of each other.

The Commission submits that it is extremely important to see the role of an unrestrained and flourishing media in helping political participation and dialogue, allowing grievances to be aired and addressed, and facilitating the hearing that public appreciation and complaints should receive (Chapter 6). More specifically the media, encouraged by governments and civil society, can convey a more constructive approach to promoting understanding; tackle causes of grievance and humiliation that underlie the appeal of extremist and instigating messages; help transcend warring boundaries and promote understanding; and develop a fuller understanding of international issues. The Commission emphasizes the importance of supporting the media in their constructive efforts – from the operation of training institutions to the actual day-to-day practice of responsible journalism.

The Commission does, of course, recognize that media portrayals can sometimes exacerbate a narrative of oppositional forces, and strengthen, rather than weaken, grievance and disaffection. The media can also, often enough, oversimplify the complexity of current problems. These dangers are there and have to be guarded against (the restraint should come primarily from the internal discipline of good journalism), but they do not, in any way, reduce the importance of the constructive role of the media in giving people more information and more understanding of each other, and also in making them more equipped to deal with potential sources of tension.

Education and young people

The Commission argues that it would be hard to exaggerate the importance of non-sectarian and non-parochial education that expands, rather than reduces, the reach of understanding and reason (Chapter 7). The Commission believes that governments should, as a matter of urgency, give priority to the necessary investment for the universal reach of well-grounded basic education. Inequality in the distribution of education shapes the incidence of exclusion, which is a source of unfairness in itself and can also be a prelude to hostility.

Educational content is crucially linked with the promotion of respect and understanding – or the opposite. The educational curriculum is central in embodying and communicating values and messages about the relationships and understandings between and across diverse identity groups related to different systems of partitioning. Knowledge of world history is particularly critical in helping to forge cosmopolitan identities, as is teaching children about the cultural heritage of a range of ethnic, racial, national, tribal and religious communities. Similarly, teaching children about the value and purpose of social cohesion based on mutual equality is another important objective. Well-designed education can also help in the adaptation of immigrants to their host or new home societies.

The interest and involvement of young people are important not only in the process of education, but also for their contribution to the development of a harmonious society. While the attention that their education demands should never be neglected, it would be a mistake to treat young people as mere recipients of the plans for their instruction made by others, rather than seeing them as thinking beings, whose concerns and enthusiasms can powerfully enrich social life.

The Commission also emphasizes the particular role of sports in which the young are commonly involved. Sport should be a vocation open to all people, irrespective of ethnicity, religion, gender or economic circumstances. Given social arrangements for special events, sport can become a reality even for those with a disability. Rigorous training and a commitment to winning medals for one's nation can help overcome many perceived divides within that nation. The Commonwealth Games, and since 2000 the

Commonwealth Youth Games, are existing institutional features in which an agenda of greater respect and understanding can helpfully find a direct place, in addition to the indirect contribution they automatically make.

Multilateral approaches

The Commission has been much guided by appreciation of the arguments behind the use of multilateral approaches and their convincing track record. Multilateral consultations and interactions can be of pervasive importance and usefulness in determining appropriate means for pursuing peace and security. The Commission attaches great importance to the Commonwealth's role in placing constructive emphasis on the use of a dialogue-based and consensus-building approach, which can better deliver benefits to all, and also deal more effectively with issues of group-based conflict in the world today.

The potential usefulness of this approach is extensive, perhaps even ubiquitous. To consider a particularly difficult case, the Commission strongly recommends that the Commonwealth's efforts in Zimbabwe must not only continue, but must be strengthened. The Commission also believes that the 'Commonwealth approach' of dialogue and consensus-building may have relevance in other parts of the world: the Commonwealth governments could usefully adopt such an approach in Iraq, where there is a huge – and growing – need for greater multilateral engagements; in Afghanistan, where the international community could strengthen the inclusive initiatives (the report discusses this issue in some detail); and in the conflicts involving Israel and Palestine, where the resumption of dialogue and the cultivation of mutual understanding are critically important. The Commission also argues that multilateralism has relevance in fighting injustice at the international level where some regions and countries have not benefited from the restructuring of the world trade system and where they continue to have little influence over decisions taken in this regard.

The Commission suggests that the Commonwealth Secretary-General's Good Offices work should be extended to address grievance internationally. More particularly, the Commission urges the Commonwealth to use its considerable experience to advocate greater use of multilateral approaches in international disputes and confrontations, working with the United Nations and other international organizations.

The reach of civil paths

Civil paths to peace, the Commission argues, are important and can be very effective. Aside from individual policies, some of which have been spelt out in some detail in the report, there is a big general need for understanding the reach and rationale of using civil paths. The need for hard security measures does not in any way reduce the abiding relevance of pursuing the civil routes.

The Commission argues, in particular, that there is a strong need for much more dialogue and discussion on the richness of human identities and the counterproductive nature of placing people in rigidly separated identity-boxes, linked with religion or community (no matter how positively each religion or each community is described). The importance of people's cosmopolitan identity also demands greater recognition than it tends to get, without denying the relevance of other identities that can comfortably co-exist with a global outlook.

At the international level, civil paths will be inescapably linked with multilateral approaches across borders. At the national level, the avoidance of sectarian divisions within a nation can be a very important component of the civil approach to peace, and the positive features of a non-divisive national political identity should get, the Commission argues, a clear and ungrudging recognition. The Secretary-General has agreed to develop a number of initiatives in consultation with Commonwealth Heads and their governments, for which we hope the resources would be forthcoming. These could helpfully build on the Commonwealth's existing work, or complement the priorities of other organizations, including those of the United Nations (such as the recommendations of the UN's Alliance of Civilizations). Such an action programme would be an important and necessary next step to the Commission's report.

Accepting diversity, respecting all human beings, and understanding the richness of perspectives that people have are of great relevance for all the Commonwealth countries, and for our 1.8 billion people. They are also important for the rest of the world. The civil paths to peace are presented here for use both inside the Commonwealth and beyond its boundaries. The Commonwealth has survived and flourished, despite the hostilities associated with past colonial history, through the use of a number of far-sighted guiding principles. The Commission argues that those principles have continuing relevance today for the future of the Commonwealth – and also for the world at large.

Amartya Sen

John Alderdice

Kwame Anthony Appiah

Adrienne Clarkson

Noeleen Heyzer

Kamal Hossain

Elaine Sihoatani Howard

Wangari Muta Maathai

Ralston Nettleford

Joan Rwabyomere

Lucy Turnbull

1. Why Do Respect and Understanding Matter?

1   Violence has been a lasting feature of human civilisation, and the contemporary world is no exception to the ubiquitous presence of assault and fury. But the world in which we live today is also one of systematic group violence, in which religious, or racial, or ethnic, or territorial divisions are used to foment violence and sometimes even genocide. Recurrent acts of targeting and terrorism make life deeply insecure for those on the 'wrong' side of the targeted separating line. Indeed, global violence clustered around systematically cultivated divisions has a huge presence in contemporary life across the world. Advances in science and technology have also increased the potentially catastrophic destruction of such violence and, as 9/11 has shown, not only in the context of nuclear, chemical or biological warfare.

2   The seriousness of global violence has led to many initiatives aimed at defeating it. Military means for trying to secure peace have been widely discussed and have sometimes also been rapidly deployed, with more reasoned and better informed justification in some cases than in others. And yet group violence through systematic instigation is not only – perhaps not even primarily – a military challenge. It is fostered in our divisive world through capturing people's minds and loyalties, and through exploiting the allegiance of those who are wholly or partly persuaded. The recruits are prodded into joining, directly or indirectly, various movements for promoting violent actions against targeted groups. Much larger numbers of people are influenced but do not take part in any violent activities themselves, contributing instead by generating

a political climate in which the most peaceful of people come to tolerate egregious acts of intolerance and brutality, on some hazily perceived grounds of 'just retaliation' or 'self-defence'.

3   Military initiatives can sometimes be of limited use, when they are well informed, well thought through, and well executed, paying attention to the diverse concerns that have to be borne in mind in any use of force. But many interventions have not met these desiderata, and – as we discuss in this report – they typically leave the root causes of violence unaddressed. They can also generate immensely counterproductive results, by creating fresh hostilities and by giving reason to distinct violent groups to join their hands in 'resisting aggression'.

4   In probing deeper into the causal processes that generate violence and into the ways and means of overcoming them, we have to examine how distortions as well as genuine misunderstandings, such as having a sense of being isolated from the 'mainstream' community, can feed extremism and violence. In alleviating the conditions that give rise to a sense of grievance and isolation through civil rather than military initiatives, and in trying to recover the ground that has already been lost, realistic processes of generating better understanding have a huge role to play. The strengthening of respect (in a very broad sense) for each other must have a critically important place in any plausible agenda for promoting peace.

5   We have to distinguish between respecting persons (including, of course, their right to hold their own views) and indiscriminately 'respecting every doctrine' held by anyone. Respecting people does not demand accepting their points of view, and a consensus to do something jointly, given the views that different people hold, does not demand that there must be unanimity of substantive views of different people.

6   Respect does, however, demand trying to understand the points of view of others and why they are held, and appreciating the shared interest that people of diverse groups have in cultivating common objectives and finding common ground, such as peace and well-being. This approach suggests a variety of practical actions that can contribute to generating resistance to violence through the social means available to us. The civil routes to peace, which this report explores and

presents, are based on a basic appreciation of the role of respect and understanding in this very broad – and constructive – sense.

What do we mean by respect and understanding?

7 In everyday life, the term 'respect' is used in a number of ways. Sometimes it refers to the esteem or honour given to senior people in acknowledgement of their greater age or experience. This denotes deference and implies a relationship that is unequal; though a distinction should be made between respect earned (for example through experience) and power taken note of (for example money or position). But in an inter-cultural context, the term 'respect!' is used quite differently – as a demand for rights and equal treatment. Here it is contrasted with disrespect – the experience of being picked upon, discriminated against, or treated in a demeaning way because, for example, of one's race, colour or culture.

8 In the context of the Commonwealth it makes sense to define respect with reference to rights and equal treatment but to broaden it beyond the issue of race so that it refers to a way of treating others, whatever their age, race, gender or other aspects of their identity, with fairness and with dignity. Looked at in this way, the term respect reflects and encapsulates the principles for which the modern Commonwealth stands – human rights, liberties, democracy, gender equality, the rule of law and a political culture that promotes transparency, accountability and economic development.

9 And respect is about acknowledging a common humanity, and a preparedness to treat everyone, no matter how different their world views, with the dignity they deserve because of their humanity. It is as much about how we treat those who occupy lower social positions as it is about how we respond to those who are more senior. There is an important distinction to make between respecting persons (and their right to hold their own views) and indiscriminately respecting what they believe in or how they behave. We can show respect to others without agreeing with their particular doctrines or their actions.

10 Understanding implies an ability to grasp what someone else is saying in order to get to the heart of what they are trying to communicate.

To do this requires a willingness to put aside one's own preconceived notions in order to appreciate their world view. Understanding, therefore, involves the acknowledgement that one's own culture and experience are not the only models for thinking or acting.

11   Like respect, understanding does not necessarily involve agreement with the views or beliefs others hold. A consensus to do something jointly therefore, given the different views that people hold, is not preconditioned by the necessity of any unanimity of view. No-one or nobody should hold a veto that requires subordination of all to a single view or belief.

12   It is also important to understand disrespect and what it is like to be disrespected. Disrespect for an individual or a community can be expressed simply through passive rejection, ignoring their presence and their needs. The poorest people – those marginalized by their poverty, social status, gender or disability – often have the least power to mobilize and make demands. Local services might be high quality but still be delivered in ways that make poor women feel like cattle, or worse. And being a woman might mean that you are all but certain to receive a sub-standard service. Being treated as invisible or irrelevant in a clinic, on a bus, or in a shop is an indication of disrespect. It is equally possible that those who are put in positions of authority can be treated with disrespect, not because of how they have behaved, but simply because they are in authority. Respect should be a characteristic of all our relations.

13   Respect and understanding are intimately connected with human rights expressed in terms of the four great freedoms (from hunger, disease, ignorance and fear) – to which one might add freedom from violent conflict. These freedoms are not attainable in a vacuum. They necessarily require consideration of the nature of basic values that underlie the actions necessary to achieve these freedoms.

Respect and understanding and the Commonwealth

14   Respect and understanding are values at the heart of what we might call the 'Commonwealth approach'. This approach involves a tradition of doing things through dialogue, where everyone has

the right to speak, to be heard and to be consulted in coming to a common view. It involves a belief in a shared process and in the ability of people – all people, no matter how diverse – to make use of that process. In essence, it is about seeking a consensus and valuing the process that brought about coming to a common view.

15   The principle of dialogue can be seen as part of respecting each other and wanting to achieve understanding rather than unilateral victory. In practice, dialogue between Commonwealth members has not always involved agreement. Indeed, the approach that has been used could even be described as getting by without an agreed perspective, but with some agreed and recognized general principles on how to do things.

16   The Declaration of Commonwealth Principles first agreed in Singapore in 1971, and then reaffirmed in Harare in 1991, reflect the importance given to respect and understanding by Commonwealth countries. These Principles emphasize the human rights of all citizens regardless of gender, race, colour, creed or political belief and the need to absolutely oppose racial prejudice and all forms of racial oppression. They recognise the urgency of economic and social development and the need to progressively remove disparities in living standards to achieve a more equitable international society. They also affirm the importance of active participation by civil society, including by women and young people, through free and democratic processes.

17   Individuals and countries of the Commonwealth have valuable experience in putting respect and understanding into practice, having played catalytic roles in helping to liberate peoples from colonialism and apartheid. The multi-ethnic and multi-religious membership of the Commonwealth embraces a diversity of faiths, cultures and societies that are marked by divisions of rich and poor, powerful and powerless, and of caste and class. The Commonwealth is therefore a microcosm of the challenges being faced in today's conflict-ridden world, but also of the determination to find solutions – not through confrontation, but through an agreement that all parties have the basic right to be fully involved in dialogue processes.

18   There are also established ways of working in the Commonwealth that have proved fundamental in putting respect and understanding

into practice. The organization seeks consensual rather than confrontational debate. It seeks out those principles on which member states can agree – whether on democracy and good governance, human rights, including those of women, or the importance of development and economic justice. It is informal and non-threatening in manner and tends to work behind the scenes in non-public ways.

19   At the same time, the wealth of non-governmental connection in the association, through Commonwealth civil society, works away at the cultural context in which these values have meaning and application, to promote respect and understanding. There are many practical examples of how Commonwealth institutions and societies contribute to a discussion and exchange of views between members of different Commonwealth countries to build respect and understanding, including between young people.[1]

20   One of the striking social changes which is currently taking place across the globe is the move from hierarchical structures to networks. We experience this dramatically in the operation of the internet, but this is merely one example of the phenomenon. The Commonwealth has always tried to operate ahead of the game in this regard since it has always operated as a network, and is therefore not only a suitable format for future international relations, but has valuable experience to share with more traditional international and intergovernmental formations.

21   That said, all Commonwealth member countries and organizations recognize the very real challenges that the Commonwealth has faced, and will continue to face, in adhering to a shared set of fundamental principles, living out these values and dealing with situations when these are flouted or abused. Over the years, there have inevitably been divergences in perspective within the Commonwealth, not least in the area of human rights. The openness of discussion and debate has sometimes brought to the surface deep divisions in perspectives that have not been resolved by extensive dialogue.

---

1 RCS, 2007. Examples include the Royal Commonwealth Society's 'Commonwealth Essay Competition' (open to all students aged between 8 and 18) and its 'Youth CHOGMs' (a simulation of the Commonwealth Heads of Government Meeting); and, the Commonwealth Policy Studies Unit's 'Commonwealth Clubs in Secondary Schools' project.

22   There is very strong support for parliamentary democracy within the Commonwealth – to a great extent inspired by the British experience but also drawing on traditions of debate and discussion in other Commonwealth countries.

23   What behaviour is or is not consistent with Commonwealth principles and values? The basis of the Commonwealth is frank and open discussion with the right of all to speak and to be heard. As a result, denying people the freedom to participate in the public life of their own country will always be in tension with membership of the Commonwealth.[2]

24   Whilst the Commonwealth does have ways of taking action against unacceptable political behaviour on the part of governments, all efforts are made to keep lines of communication open (for example with countries under suspension). This is to ensure that there remain channels for supporting the efforts of those within a country who are struggling to re-establish democratic practice and respect.

25   In many countries the Commonwealth approach to dialogue has yielded significant and positive results and has even achieved consensus across previously entrenched divisions. South Africa's peaceful transition from apartheid to a modern democracy is a powerful example of the approach in action, not least in ensuring that previous critics of sanctions against a white minority-rule regime were brought around to support a common strategy. Also, as we discuss further in paragraphs 224–226, had greater priority been given to an interactive civil approach after the initial defeat of the Taliban regime in Afghanistan, some of the residual problems there might have been avoided, which have instead resurfaced and grown stronger over the years.

Why do respect and understanding matter now?

26   Respect and understanding matter now for three important reasons that drive the timeliness of this report:

- Firstly, because of the prevalence and the far-reaching effects of violent conflict in the world today and the apparent persistence

---

2 Sen, 1998.

of conflict even as, or perhaps because, the world grows more interconnected.

- Secondly, respect and understanding in the world is critical now because of the persistence of terrorism and the fear of terrorism.
- Thirdly, as we have already noted above, our increased technological capacity for destruction through ever-more sophisticated and powerful weapons of war makes the avoidance of human and environmental catastrophe as a result of war a matter of profound urgency.

27   Violence is deeply disturbing and even low-level violence at a community level has enormous impacts. Fear of its continuation may stop people going to work or sending their children to school; relations of trust between neighbours may break down, further isolating vulnerable groups such as the elderly. If the police move in clumsily, or act in a way seen to be partisan, then the risk of violence is likely to increase – with the police also seen as potential perpetrators. In the longer term, violence damages the whole economy – for example, through reducing inward investment, raising the cost of doing business and removing the skills and the savings of those who can afford to move away.

28   Violent conflict also takes a huge toll on the poor and on the prospects for reducing poverty. Of the 34 countries currently furthest from reaching the Millennium Development Goals (MDGs), 22 are in the midst of, or emerging from, violent conflict. The consequences usually fall most heavily on women and children, who make up the majority of displaced people – at times of violent conflict women and girls often experience rape, sexual violence, forced pregnancy, kidnap and abuse.

29   The Commonwealth is not immune to conflicts within and between its member countries. At the end of 2003 nearly half of the 23 armed conflicts between and within states around the world were in Commonwealth countries. The Commonwealth has extensive experience in addressing conflicts, and, more importantly, defusing the tensions that create them.

30   Respect and understanding in the world are critical now because of the persistence of terrorism and the fear of terrorism. Some of

the ways in which this is being tackled seem to have the effect of provoking, not reducing, violence and terrorist acts. A new, or at least a complementary approach, is urgently needed.

31 The Commission is persuaded that some of the policy actions taken to protect citizens from further terrorist attacks have been limited in their conceptualisation and in their effectiveness. Because of the importance given by all governments to the threat of terrorism today it is worth setting out our understanding of the limitations of current approaches.

The so-called 'War on Terror'

32 Current approaches to the 'War on Terror' raise many questions on a number of fronts. Most importantly, there has been a tendency to see terrorism as essentially a military or security threat requiring, primarily, a military and security response. Where a military intervention has been tried and there has been an effort to effect democracy by military means, as in the case of Iraq, it has not succeeded either in military terms or in terms of leaders being able to maintain the support for a sustained intervention by their publics at home or internationally. In Afghanistan, where the rationale for intervention was to remove a regime that posed a threat to international peace and security through its extensive support of terrorism, efforts to establish a new democratic constitution – which would have been challenging enough in any circumstances – have been undermined by the diversion of resources to Iraq.

33 World public opinion has taken a dim view of this approach and has raised many questions, not least whether the war on terror itself is helping to sustain feelings of grievance and therefore contributing to the possibility of future attacks, as well as to a higher level of violence in countries like Afghanistan, Pakistan and Iraq. There have been many unintended consequences of adopting the strategy of a 'War on Terror,' not least that aspects of the strategy seem to have further inflamed sentiment across the world. Not surprisingly, there has been a loss of hope and a growing cynicism about a felt loss of the common international values and standards that all nations in principle adhere to.

34   It could be argued that, in Britain and America, attempts at engaging against terrorism through the medium of faith and religion have had, at times, a perverse effect of magnifying the voice of extremist Islamists at a time when the political and civil roles of Muslims in civil society, including in the practice of democracy, need emphasis and much greater support. Faith-based approaches make it more difficult for politically secular Muslims (who do not have any standing, or any great urge, to speak in a faith-based discussion) to speak out against terrorism and violence. Like everyone else, they feel 'voiceless' in the middle of faith-based discussions. Religious extremism has made citizens, whatever their religious affiliation, less capable of taking responsible political action and speaking out against violence. And this tendency has often been strengthened rather than weakened by attempts to combat terrorism through recruiting the religious establishments of various communities to 'the right side', with young people being dismissive of the older religious establishment spokesman when they line up with Western governments. Civil society is currently in need of strengthening with all the positive resources at our disposal. Whilst religious identities can be used in a very positive way, by for example instilling a moral code and way of living, stressing religious identities over and above other political and social identities can undermine efforts to strengthen civil society and community cohesion. The culturally rich, more nuanced non-religious aspects of pluralism have been downplayed at precisely the wrong moment. This makes it easier for belligerent extremists to gather support and gain a stronger foothold in many countries.

35   There have been other casualties of the strategy of the 'War on Terror'. In countries that have themselves experienced terrorist attacks, greatly enhanced additional surveillance operations and a raft of new counter-terrorism laws have raised questions about the state's ability to uphold the rule of law and individual rights. The difficulty is the balance these new measures and laws must achieve to allow policing and security agencies to find and prosecute suspects for criminal offences, whilst maintaining legal safeguards in the criminal justice system that protect individual freedoms and uphold the rule of law.

36 A major concern is that the strategy of a 'War on Terror' may be helping to increase support for the messages of oppression, humiliation and disrespect that groups involved in terror attacks are putting forward. Where state responses have included extra-judicial measures that allow the government to circumvent national or international law, or if the military response is seen as disproportionate and is interpreted as vengeance, or if the measures proposed to tackle terrorism are seen as simply unworkable then, almost perversely, this can increase public support for the message, if not the methods, of the insurgents. People may abhor the use of terror tactics but nonetheless have some sympathy for those who seem to be subjected to laws which they perceive to be harsh and undemocratic, and as a result show concern for the rights of these people as a means of expressing their opposition to the impacts of counter-terrorism strategies. The public can be antagonized by the adverse impact of official reactive security measures, especially if they are not proportionate. On the one hand, the Commission accepts and endorses the importance of effective security measures for the prevention of violent crime, no matter how generated. The strength of security which we firmly support must not, however, be confused with an image of indiscriminate toughness that gives people a false sense of security.

37 Terror attacks carried out in the name of a particular identity inevitably have the potential to polarize societies. Sadly, counter-terrorism strategies can themselves exacerbate this polarization. The threat of terrorism following 9/11 fostered particular resentment of perceived migrants in many countries, particularly migrants of Muslim origin.[3] The response of many Muslims was to retreat from public discourse at exactly the moment that more Muslim voices were needed. When new security measures are imposed quickly following a terror attack, without due debate, discussion and sensitivity, this can further divide people at a time when more engagement is what is required.

38 Those communities perceived to share an aspect of their identity with the perpetrators are then particularly vulnerable. Increases in hate-related violent attacks against minorities are extensively

3 UN DESA, 2004: 2.

documented for all countries that have experienced terrorism. Efforts to protect and reassure minority communities – who often feel acutely vulnerable – that are carried out through community policing strategies and dialogue with community leaders, have greatly helped. But the problem could be better mitigated by a response which simultaneously consults with minorities, community groups and civil society about the short and long-term consequences of all aspects of counter-terrorism action at the same time as taking reasonable, well-conceived and well-communicated security measures, both internal and external.

39   Terrorism is not simply like other forms of political violence. The Commission sees terrorism as a tactic – as well as a crime. It may be used by the left or the right, or by populist or nationalist extremists. It involves the premeditated use of violence to create a climate of fear, but is aimed at a wider target than the immediate victims of the violence. The victims may have symbolic significance but the real target is not the victim. The target is the 'responsible authority', for example a government or a dominant group. The aim of many terrorist groups is to force a reaction – or overreaction – by the responsible authority toward terrorist acts and those who perpetrate them. It is this (over)reaction that makes it possible to cast the government or responsible authority as the greater villain.

40   The 'responsible authority' (or its historic predecessors) is seen as having perpetrated an injustice. Terrorists and their supporters see themselves as righting some terrible wrong, some humiliation, some deep disrespect that has been done to them, their community or their nation by an authoritarian government or state. Terrorists and their supporters believe that they are 'freedom fighters', embarking with great courage and risk to themselves on a heroic task, namely of righting that perceived wrong.

41   Yet the nature of this injustice, the 'terrible wrong' that they aspire to right, is under-explored. There is a disinclination to understand – never mind talk to – those involved because of the means through which their grievances are expressed. The tendency at national level to exclude groups classified as terrorists from the political process, through listing them in Terrorism Acts and Criminal Codes, is the antithesis of a process based on dialogue. Where dialogue is

possible, and where the stated aim of terrorists is ending repression and humiliation and having a greater level of inclusion in society and its political processes, then dialogue is essential – as hard as that is to engage in where there is violence and fear. Where it may not be possible is where there is a militant goal to destroy a democratic society or way of life based on the rule of law. In that case, it is essential to create the conditions where there is less capacity for extremists to win the hearts and minds of others to their cause: that can only be done through creating the perception that it is possible for members of minorities to feel included in society and to have a shared sense of destiny in a common future.

42 Dialogue with groups at the far ends of the political spectrum, or with those that hold views that most people feel are repugnant, is a probing and uncomfortable test for countries that have experienced terrorism. Yet it must be done, or tried, where the objectives of the terrorists do not include the complete destruction of a democratic state governed by the rule of law. Whilst not underestimating the difficulties of the Commonwealth experience, the fundamental truth is that the willingness to listen and engage in dialogue not only helps but is the only way to bring any form of political violence to a sustainable end. It also addresses the criticism that peace is unlikely without addressing justice.

Understanding root causes better requires challenging various cultural theories

43 The tendency to present the causes of conflict or terrorism as having their roots in a clash of civilisations has seized the popular imagination. The Commission believes such cultural theories to be deeply flawed on a conceptual level and deeply divisive in practice.

44 For one thing, separating the world into discrete civilisations assumes that: (a) the millions of individuals classified under each categorization identify with the persona they are 'given', and (b) there is sufficient homogeneity within each identified group for the categorization to mean something.

45   Furthermore, these cultural theories have tended to presume that the groups so identified will inevitably clash. The Commission categorically rejects this claim. There is simply no substantial evidence for it. Millions of people may be represented as being either part of 'the Islamic world' or 'the West' (to take two examples of such cultural categories), but neither Muslims nor Westerners think, act or believe as one. Individuals within these hugely differentiated population groups have multiple affiliations, multiple identities. There is as much discrepancy in belief, political position and cultural practices within the populations referred to as between them.

46   Being Muslim or Western can never be an overarching identity that determines everything that a person believes in or is prepared to do. It is imperative that world leaders are not seduced into thinking that these categories, representing as they do such a diverse range of peoples, accurately capture the feelings and values of those so categorized, much less that they have the power to 'explain' violence. Reducing people to such categories represents only part of them, rather than the whole persons they are, and fails to recognize the complexity of their diverse affiliations and identities.[4]

47   Taking up this challenge now is vital: theories such as the 'clash of civilisations' are already widely reflected in the press and have found their way into a range of explanatory frameworks that in turn influence public policy. They will inevitably find their way into classroom discussions and, ultimately, textbooks, thus institutionalizing a way of thinking that will indirectly influence young people. For the Commonwealth, it is also important to avoid inadvertent regressions to a divisive mindset.[5]

48   The issues discussed in this report are therefore substantial concerns in their own right across the world. The Commonwealth is no exception in feeling the consequences of greater sensitivity about ethnic and religious identity, and the effects of the failure to tackle grievances.

49   This report operates within this larger context, which itself is constantly evolving and developing, in part through the work of

---

4 On this see Sen, 1999 and Sen, 2006.
5 On this see Appiah, 2006. See also Appiah, 2004 and Sen, 2006.

governments and international organizations, to address underlying issues. Indeed, even with a robust and shared understanding of the problem, it is important that those holding political and economic power implement appropriate remedies to the fullest extent that they are able. This will require additional effort to ensure that:

- The rationales for intervention in particular situations are clear and demonstrable, and are thus more likely to promote consensus (or more near-consensus) about what needs to be done.

- The potential responses are viewed within the framework of various existing Commonwealth and inter-governmental objectives (including ending violent conflict, promoting development, extending democracy, addressing sustainability, tackling extremism and identifying the root causes of radicalization).

- There are better understandings of emerging challenges, for example through policies aimed at targeting highly disengaged groups who are at risk of sinking into deeper and/or further kinds of alienation.

- Governments in particular appreciate their own limitations and fully recognize the role that others (such as the business and civil society communities) can play. The influence of neighbouring giants or regional superpowers, the mass media and market behaviour may mean that a particular governments' role is limited in any case.

- Important gaps in knowledge and understanding are flagged, in order to establish priorities for follow-up work among practitioners and also among researchers.

50 With the above caveats in mind, it is important still to remember that in many cases there is much more that governments can do to secure greater respect and understanding. This must of course never involve turning a blind eye to gross discrimination and victimization. It might involve articulating clearly that government itself stands for the principles of respect for individuals as human beings, and that all people have the right to be treated fairly and with dignity. Government can also: (a) adopt policies that tackle gross unfairness and injustice, (b) create systems which give

citizens and their preferences a strong voice, and (c) acknowledge the role of the international community in shaping universal values and promoting positive change.

51   There are other things that governments can do, in policy-making in many areas, to develop the sorts of connections across groups that are so crucial to avoiding conflict. Even the operation of the military can contribute to this. Armies and police forces provide a crucial mechanism by which people of diverse origins can be brought together in a context that enhances respect and understanding. Most people enter the armed or police forces when young. Their attitudes are still forming. And the military and the police are institutions that, by their nature, must exercise more control over the lives and attitudes of its members than any other government bodies. Strict insistence on non-discrimination, promotion without regard to ethnicity, and the principle that all must be willing to take orders from superiors, whatever their social origin, creates a context in which even those who may enter with discriminatory attitudes can often be persuaded to change them for the better. The approach of the military in dealing with people in the communities in which they work is also vital. More than ever the real military struggle is for the hearts and minds of people rather than simply for control of territory, and this requires a very different set of skills. A serious long-term commitment to sport in multi-ethnic teams can have similar good effects.

52   Social psychologists confirm what common sense suggests: people who work together when young in circumstances of equality and mutual dependence across races, religions and ethnicities, tend to be less prejudiced than those who do not.[6] Similarly, in the area of employment, integrating government workplaces and enforcing anti-discrimination laws in the private sector can lead to developing cross-group linkages outside the workplace.[7] In the context of educational policy, encouraging young people not only to study together but to play sports, engage in community activities, make music, and otherwise work together across groups, can have similar beneficial effects. In all these cases – the military,

---

6 Moskos, 1986.
7 Estlund, 2003.

government and private sector employment, and education – there are opportunities to shape policies and develop practical proposals that will encourage respect and understanding.

53 Although others have an important role to play, the role of government in supporting respect and understanding is unique. For one thing, despite obstacles, it is often much better placed to provide standards of equality and equal treatment. Government can also pursue strategic public policy goals to remedy unfairness and injustice. And, of course, properly accountable government is in a position to be answerable for its actions and inactions.

2. The Nature and Nurture of Violence

The nature of violence

54　Violence is the most recognizable form of disrespect, a very public indicator that respect and understanding have broken down. It takes many forms but it is useful to make two sorts of distinction:

- First, between violence carried out in the course of ordinary crime for personal gain (robbery and the like) and political violence. Our concern is with the second, but the first is also important as robbery itself shows intense disrespect to the person whose property is looted or stolen or whose person is harmed. Nor are ordinary crime and political violence necessarily distinct, the two can merge: the overall cause of the leaders may be political but their supporters and followers may act with a mix of personal motives (looting can be for monetary advantage, acts of atrocity or honour can be carried out to enhance personal status, and organized crime pursued as a way to finance an illegal insurgency or terrorist campaign).

- The second necessary distinction is between violence that is primarily physical and violence that involves no physical contact but can have deep psychological effects. Violence of this sort can manifest itself as a form of intense yet unspoken disregard. The poorest people, those marginalized by their poverty, social status, gender, age or disability, tend to experience this form of 'violent disrespect' most intensely. It is communicated simply through passive rejection of their existence – by being treated as invisible or irrelevant in everyday life. It is often evident where inequalities are endemic and have become institutionalized; unfair treatment then becomes part of the social structure.[1]

- Physical and psychological violence are often combined. Violence is rarely 'just' a physical attack aimed at causing hurt or pain. It is also an attack on personhood, on the human-ness of others, on an individual, community or institution's sense of self-worth, on identity.

- The rape of women in war is an extreme example of an attack on personhood. Whilst it is a physical act that aims to cause individual women physical and mental pain, it is also a symbolic act that reflects the notion of women as embodiments of national and cultural identity that can be violated through their bodies. Violence against women is, therefore, aimed at destroying the honour and self-respect of the whole group, not alone in the present, but because of the special role of women in bearing the next generation, a destruction of the hopes for the future.

55 Violence of these types, although important in many contexts, and as we have noted frequently symbolic in various respects, has to be distinguished from the violence associated with terrorism. The victims of terrorist attacks may be the terrorist's own community or even his or her own body but the target is authority. Terrorist forms of violence intentionally break basic human codes of conduct, so that by violating all social norms it provokes outrage and cannot be ignored. The motives can be complex: through his or her actions, a terrorist may be trying to force concessions, affect public opinion, or bring attention to their cause. It may even be an act of desperation. But in some cases, there is undeniably a much stronger symbolic aspect: the organizationally 'weak' terrorist group aims, in addition to drawing attention to their own injustice, to provoke the 'strong' authorities into a substantial overreaction that will damage their standing and moral authority both domestically and internationally.

56 Those who are most disadvantaged may even internalize their disadvantage and feel a sense of worthlessness; whilst acutely aware of their position they may be profoundly disempowered by

---

1 For example, dalits (scheduled castes), tribals (scheduled tribes), other castes and Muslims who are poor and disadvantaged face serious levels of exclusion in some South Asian countries in terms of their access to income, education, social services and their participation in political and decision-making processes.

it, particularly if previous attempts to change their status came to nothing. They may endure their situation without protest in case their demand for justice incites worse repression. This form of violence is rarely heralded by loud protest. It is endured by millions the world over as part of the 'normal' order of things.

57   Some of the most entrenched social, economic, political and cultural injustices are endured by women, half the world's population. Young people may also be ignored as they also tend not to be the leaders of their communities or to have a voice in their institutions. They therefore lack the power to shape agendas. Even when their voices are heard they are not always systematically mainstreamed into national debates. Women and young people have to struggle particularly hard to command respect in countries where principles of patriarchy and seniority determine who holds power, and the damage suffered is transmitted inter-generationally. Again, this exclusion is not violence in a physical sense but a violation of their right to be heard and respected, which supplements the iniquity and barbarity of actual physical and sexual violence and abuse against women and young people by men. This is a priority issue in making the world a more just place.

The nurture of violence

58   Political violence is nurtured by psychological as well as physical factors. For violence to be sustained the 'other side' must be seen as not only different but also associated with beliefs or actions felt to be inimical to a way of life or dearly held values. In short, the other side must be seen as a threat. Violence against the other can then be presented as protecting one's own way of life. If violence is seen as a form of self-defence ordinary people are more likely to accept it as morally justified.

59   A first and concerning step on the road to violence is, therefore, the truncating of identities down to a single category. It is not hard to see how this helps to draw potential battle lines. One of the most frequently used means of creating in-group solidarity comes from framing the out-group as threatening, parasitic or worse (a form of 'scapegoating'). Such sentiments take hold by denying the

commonality of experience and interest that lies across and between groups. In the case of systematic, organized sectarian violence, this element becomes central to the ability of leaders to rally supporters and target a single common foe.

60   Two observations stand out when contemplating this problem in its severest form:

- The first is that extreme circumstances are hallmarked by a politics that rejects negotiation. That is to say, one side's willingness to discuss and negotiate the shape of the grievance or concern of the other side is completely undermined by their inability to see the other side in terms that are recognizable or have inherent value. The most extreme version, of course, is to portray the other side in non-human terms, thus obviating the need to justify hatred or violence.

- The second observation is that one-dimensional identity is fundamentally flattening in its purpose and in its outcomes. It is designed to deliver an all-powerful lens through which the world is seen, though not required to be understood. Wearers of the lens are provided with a world-view that is sufficiently all encompassing to relegate individual choice to the margins. In extreme conditions, it supplies a plentiful source of nourishment to build and sustain hatred. The odds against mutuality, or interlocking lines of empathy and solidarity, are heavy stacked as a consequence.

Identity politics and its distortion

61   The rise of identity politics of this kind is far from new. Even in modern times, there are no shortages of vivid illustrations of powerful, exclusionary hate-driven identity politics and movements that have denied even the most minimal value to others. National Socialism in Germany in the mid-twentieth century is arguably the most well-documented example. The partition of India in the 1940s was characterized by the same elements, most notably the sudden evaporation – and denial, in many cases – of cross-community links and bonds. And the chapter of African slavery in the New World (to say nothing of the related chapter of

indentured labour throughout the European imperial world) from the sixteenth to nineteenth centuries, is a compelling example of the assignment of one racial identity as a means of creating political and cultural dominance.

62   But, even putting these large examples to one side, it is equally important to note a general trend towards the growth of one-dimensional identity politics and fundamentalism. This has been observed both in the developed and developing worlds. As a partial result of (a negative reaction to) globalization, it has meant that particular kinds of identity-based conflict are now much more rapidly projected in a range of otherwise quite dissimilar societies. For instance, contentious and campaigning forms of collective identity have emerged in recent years that centre on opposition to the potentially 'homogenizing forces of globalization'. These identities have found it relatively easy to fuse or find common cause with related concerns about the economic domination of global corporations, threats of environmental degradation and failure to tackle perceived regional injustices. Campaigns of opposition to all of these things often converge, and people with very different views campaign together against the authorities who they regard as being 'to blame', though often for quite opposite reasons.

63   One-dimensional identities are particularly nurtured where an overarching value system is put forward to justify the basis for being against each and all of these forces. The narrative of anti-globalization movements is a simple, ready-made way of supplying such a narrative, and this has had remarkably powerful effects in shaping a sense of common understanding. Given that the dynamics of a globalized economy are far from being perfectly understood, it is clear that this reaction is actually an emotional rather than an intellectual response, with fear being the dominant emotion involved. Nevertheless, a form of single dimension of identity has emerged that has been impressive in appealing to the multiple identities that underpin concern and opposition to various aspects of globalization. It is striking that a number of anti-globalization movements have been effective in doing just this.

Faith and identity

64   Faith has always been a particularly powerful force in the construction of identity. Faith is often a force for good; the values of all of the main faiths of the world promote love and understanding, respect and hope, care by the strong for the weak, and societies based on justice, fairness, co-existence and harmony.[2]

65   The Commonwealth Foundation has recently launched an innovative project examining faith, development and social cohesion. It aims to:

- encourage debate and advance learning about collaboration between faith-based groupings in addressing development and social issues, and
- investigate the value and relevance of inter-religious co-operation, and particularly the roles this can play in helping to address development and social issues.

66   This initiative centres on perspectives (mainly drawn from a non-governmental background) on inter-religious co-operation. These are used to stimulate further debate on the scope and potential for inter-religious co-operation for greater social cohesion. It represents a basic building block of mutual respect and understanding across traditional boundaries.

67   However, faith has also been used throughout history to promote the interests of those with destructive aims. As a legitimising discourse for violence, faith has an advantage over purely political ideologies because of its ability to justify, inspire, empower – and not be proved wrong. This is due to the transcendental nature of belief ('fighting injustice is God's will'), the inspiration of religious hope ('God will fulfil His promises') and the centrality of faith ('no matter how bad things get, this is the Right Way'). Fearful believers may come to accept, if only inadvertently, a 'politically activist theology of violence', which usually means reconciling 'a single, simultaneously loving and violent God'.

68   Convinced by their leaders that their way of life or their belief system is both superior to others and is allegedly 'supported

---

2 Clarke, 2006.

by God', they can be easily persuaded that their fundamental values and way of life is under threat. Once this threat has been internalized and a powerful sense of fear generated, it is a small step to believing that violence is justified and that a war must be waged to preserve the way of life that has been pre-ordained for them. As several authors observe, secular ideas can also be held religiously – extreme nationalism, communism and fascism have functioned religiously insofar as adherents are passionate in their conviction and motivation and are prepared to die, but also to kill, for their beliefs.

69   This is particularly pertinent today as leaders use single identity categorizations of the world to garner support for wider missions that have to do with their own bid for political and economic power, nationally and internationally. Leaders for whom their own political positioning is a primary goal will inevitably play down the identities and interests that 'their' group shares with others. They well know that it is when people come together on the basis of identities outside constructed dualisms – when they meet and act as women, as young people, as citizens of a state or as people who share a regional identity, a political outlook or an artistic interest – that relationships based on mutual understanding develop, that violence is eschewed, and respect comes to characterise their interactions. Violence cannot be maintained between those who understand and respect each other. It can only be sustained with a breakdown of respect and understanding.

70   It is these multiple identities and this sort of connectedness that the Commonwealth represents and that it tries to support through its different activities. From the Commonwealth perspective, each nation is first and foremost a society of individuals that have multiple sources of affiliation and many bases of relating to each other.

71   The aim in future must be to strive even harder to recognize and nurture connections between groups on the basis of their multiple identities in order to avoid the pressure of being coalesced into polarized worlds. Efforts can be made at many levels. The starting point is personal awareness. Each of us can resist the tendency of identity politics to ignore the complexity and multiplicity of our

identities through broadening our understanding of the richness of human identity. A Hutu who is roused to hostility against a Tutsi can be reminded that they are both Rwandans, both Africans, perhaps even both Kigalians. He should be asked to recognize, too, that they share a human identity. Even though the British, French and Germans tore each other apart in 1914–1918, they now recognize each other, with little difficulty, as fellow Europeans.

3. Poverty, Inequality and Humiliation

Poverty and inequality – links to violence

72 There has been a great deal of debate about the linkages between disadvantage and discord. Various causal relationships have been suggested and explored in respect of a wide variety of conflicts. Some are more persuasive than others, but none, we believe, are compelling. The fundamental point is that, since even extreme poverty by itself does not necessarily lead to violence, where violence does occur other further factors must be in play.

73 Poverty needs to be addressed in its own right and on the basis of commitments made by individual countries and the international community to achieve the Millennium Development Goals. But poverty alone does not automatically make people violent nor, in particular, does it lead to terrorism.

74 To illustrate that poverty is rarely single-handedly responsible for group violence it is instructive to consider the connections between these phenomena in Northern Ireland, Britain and Calcutta (Kolkata), India. Successful efforts to reduce economic inequalities in Northern Ireland during the 1970s and 1980s did not greatly impact in the short term on the course of the Troubles. Although they helped to assuage some Catholic grievances on the economic and social fronts, these policies did little to address the essentially political grievances of the Catholic/Nationalists, which were about the very legitimacy of the state itself. At the same time they antagonized Loyalist/Protestants (some of whom were also disadvantaged) who felt themselves being surreptitiously betrayed by the British.

75   In Britain, for example, opening up new economic opportunities in economically disadvantaged areas will not necessarily assuage feelings of alienation and grievance amongst black young people in inner urban areas who do not have access to good schools and employment-related networks. They are five times more likely to be stopped and searched by the police in London than are white young people.[1] Here, the actual problem is the perception of discrimination and disrespect in policing policy which cannot be overcome without a real partnership being established between the community and those who police the community.

76   Kolkata is one of the poorest cities in India –in the world, even. However, it also has a very low crime rate – the lowest crime rate of any Indian city. This applies to the incidence of murder as well as to all other crimes. It also applies to crime against women, the incidence of which is very substantially lower than in any other Indian city.[2]

77   Crime is not an easy subject to explain with empirical generalizations, but there are some possible connections. One is that Kolkata has benefited from the fact that it has a long history of being a thoroughly mixed city where neighbourhoods have not been separated on ethnic or religious lines, as has occurred elsewhere. There are also other social influences, such as the huge role of shared cultural activities in the city, which mobilize the residents in co-operative directions.

78   The politics of the city may also play a part. The focus of left-leaning politics in Kolkata and West Bengal on deprivation related to class, and more recently gender, has made it harder to exploit religious differences to instigate riots against minorities, as has happened elsewhere – for example against Muslims and Sikhs in Bombay and Ahmedabad. Cultural and social factors (and sometimes the absence of such factors), as well as features of political economy, are therefore important in understanding violence in the world today; they demand integrated attention as they are rarely separable.

79   More direct than the relationship between poverty and violence are the links between inequality, particularly economic inequality, and violence. There are a number of reasons why socio-economic

1 Stewart, 2005: 7.
2 National Crime Records Bureau, Government of India 2006: 53 (table 1.8).

marginalization or disadvantage can be linked to patterns of violent conflict. These will normally relate to both subjectively perceived and objectively measured material inequalities, and a sense of injustice about those inequalities, as well as to a combination of other factors that are specific to the situation.

80   Objective as well as perceived disadvantage can interplay with one another. Thus, one group has, or is perceived to have, the land, the well-paid jobs, the best services, and the other has very limited access to these. In other words we need to assess the evenness or unevenness of the opportunity structures that exist and to take a long look at how far access and outcomes are, or can become, open to weaker groups. Patterns of disadvantage may be to do with discrimination (in jobs, housing), long-institutionalized cultural attitudes and structural inequalities (racism, the legacy of migration, lack of citizenship status), the apparent lack of government moves to put in place policies and laws to redress these inequalities, or other causes.

Rationales for intervention

81   What matters from the perspective of public policy is the degree to which inequality, particularly where it is deeply ingrained over time, can be tackled by extending opportunity structures.

82   In these circumstances the state should intervene to, in effect, represent and sponsor the interests of the powerless.

83   When socio-economic inequality is widely evident, acknowledged, and linked to opportunity structures, interventions can aim to correct economic distortions or deliver a fairer outcome. For example, the exclusion of a specific group from particular labour market opportunities may be experienced in daily terms as discrimination. Enlightened public policy can correct the current poor use of labour, which disadvantages both those who experience discrimination and the society as a whole, which is damaged by structural inequality and unfairness.

84   The public interest, crudely speaking, lies in bearing down on discriminatory and exclusionary practices in order to deliver

benefits for the excluded or oppressed group (arguably helpful to the group) and all groups (compelling in the interests of all). The short-run loss of benefits for advantaged groups is something that must be managed in the meantime, perhaps through cushioning devices and open explanation and dialogue, if an adverse reaction is not to occur.

85   The first task in tackling inequality is to acknowledge that it exists. There must be a common, shared understanding of the problem.

Embedded inequality can be harder to tackle

86   Inequalities are more consequential when they are clearly perceived and linked with other divisions. Purely economic measures of inequality, such as the degree of disparity between the wealthiest and poorest groups in a society, are aggravated when minorities are disproportionately represented at the lower end of the economic scale. For example, when the people in the bottom groups in terms of income have different non-economic characteristics, in terms of race (such as being black rather than white), or immigration status (such as being recent arrivals rather than older residents), then the significance of the economic inequality is substantially magnified by its coupling with other divisions.

87   Unrest often reflects the strong effects of such coupling (for example, in the turmoil in the periphery of Paris, France and other cities in the autumn of 2005). The same degree of economic inequality may be much more explosive in one case than in another, when it occurs in combination with disparities in other social characteristics. In a global context, the proliferation of satellite television means that people in many poorer nations have a window into the lives of those in richer countries, and see the difference.

88   Violence, when it erupts, can seem mis-targeted when it is not directed at the obvious suspects (the government, large global corporations such as mining and oil companies), but instead at other groups in the area – those who are poor too but are seen to be benefiting in a local context and even if only marginally – from the presence of global corporations. Battles for 'crumbs from the table'

may also have historical roots – the unequal distribution today of mineral wealth reignites the memory of previous imbalances. Where people of particular sub-groups have greater access to these 'crumbs', this inequality must be diluted through opening up educational and vocational opportunities.

89 Perceptions of inequality can, paradoxically, also be felt by the relatively powerful, not just the relatively powerless. In this case the issue is generally a fear of losing control of a resource to which they have previously had access or about which they have a sense of entitlement.

90 This accounts for the antipathy of existing residents towards newly arrived migrants in the same economic class ('they are after our jobs'), to say nothing of existing settled migrants who face new competition for scarce resources. Not surprisingly, this antipathy is greater if the existing residents are poor themselves and have had to struggle to get a foothold in the job market. The last thing they want is to give up this tenuous position to people who will accept even lower wages. Their own loss is seen as directly caused by the gain of others.

91 Violence is therefore often occasioned by a fear of losing out on something. State violence also falls into this category. When the police or army are ordered to fire on crowds of demonstrators it is often because the government is already on the back foot. The violence is instrumental – it is used to suppress opposition but also to inspire fear, all in the name of regaining or maintaining political control.

92 Yet inequality, even severe inequality, does not inevitably lead to violence or, necessarily, even to protest. Huge inequalities exist between groups that live together without incident. This may be because the inequality has been internalized and the minority group feels its position is 'natural'. It may also be because they are aware of the inequality but do not make an issue of it – perhaps they are recent migrants and are prepared to put up with hardship because they hope for betterment in the future and for the sake of their children (which can store up problems which arise in the second and third generation of immigrant families).

93   Lack of protest may also be for pragmatic reasons; if protest has been tried before and met with a violent response then putting up with inequality may be a choice. Perhaps the growth of the economy and the prospect of educational advancement inspire hope. If the minority group can appeal to existing mechanisms for complaint and redress – if the political process allows for voice and the courts work well – inequality may be countenanced in the belief that their voice will be heard and their situation improved in the longer term. The Commission is keen to stress that objective material inequality does not mean people automatically protest, let alone choose violence.

Triggers for violence will vary

94   So what additional factors are normally present when violent conflict occurs? And how is violence sustained, given its enormously destructive impacts – for individuals, for communities, for nations? We have already alluded to one often missed element: the way in which various identities are truncated to one dimension which is then understood and presented as a fundamental clash of values, civilisations or belief systems.

95   In short, it is only with instigation that a grievance (for example over the unequal distribution of a resource) comes to be interpreted as an attack on the identity of a group. The message that must be conveyed and take root is: (a) 'This is happening because you are Kurds or Shias, Catholics or Protestants, Kosovars' – or whoever – and (b) 'There is no way of defending what is ours (and our self-respect) other than through violence'.

96   One of the legacies of colonialism is that it left in place populations already demarcated in terms of single identities and therefore potentially open to this sort of message. In many post-colonial countries racial, ethnic, and religious identities became politically and legally institutionalized through deliberate and planned processes of decolonization and nation-building, resulting in clearly differentiated populations within bounded categories of identity, as well as simple distinctions of majority and minority.

97 In many of these countries, group privilege and rights were and continue to be officially entrenched in the institutions, processes, and practices of the nation-state, thereby reproducing multiple disparities among groups who have been classified and administered as distinct and unequal. In such circumstances group mobilization can easily take place along the fault-lines of identity.

But humiliation can also have links to disrespect and violence

98 Feelings of humiliation can also be powerful contributors to a sense of disrespect and grievance. Humiliation is born from current or remembered ill-treatment, often over decades and even centuries, so that after some time people's energy and self-esteem ebbs away. Their sense of what is right is no longer taken into account and they are left with a sense of acute injustice. Violence that is underlain by feelings of humiliation and shaming can be experienced as a form of retaliation, a fighting back for self-esteem and a statement of self-worth.

99 There are many examples of how humiliation has been imposed on peoples and communities and on how it has (though not always) lead to retaliatory action.

100 The Independent Commission on Africa led by Albert Tevoedjre argued in their 2003 report that Africa is a 'continent of humiliation'. They considered the factors that have made for its subjugation and denigration over the last millennium. These include the transatlantic slave trade, the colonization process and the fragmentation of the continent before and during the colonial period, the systematic devaluation of Africa's natural and human resources through an unjust exchange system and the portrayal of Africa as a continent of poverty in the media. While addressing underlying causes is essential, the Tevoedjre Report also sees winning the 'war against humiliation' as the primary task for Africa in this millennium, through institution – and capacity-building and empowerment.[3]

101 The narrative of humiliation that is articulated and received in many Muslim societies is an important theme amongst commentators

---

3 Tevoedjre, 2002.

analysing the root causes of growing Islamist fervour. Some have gone further and sought to explain today's tensions in terms of a sense of collective humiliation felt by declining Islamic empires from the sixteenth century onwards. Even the most casual observer acknowledges the contemporary dynamics of global Islam in which the sense of the honour or dignity of Muslims is under attack. A perception of humiliation at the hands of western, secularly-minded governments and publics is a core element of the narrative.

102 In a similar vein the Palestinian readiness to be recruited for violent 'retaliation' against Israel is made possible by the sense of humiliation which has been caused by displacement, and a sense of oppression and statelessness.

103 Migrant populations, those that have moved from their place of origin either through their own volition, through forceful removal or through their vulnerability to poverty and unequal treatment may also feel a sense of individual or group humiliation. This can occur however short the journey. Migrants who are not afforded the rights of citizens and who have an identity as 'non-persons', who feel their energy and enthusiasm and skills are consistently ignored when they try to find work or housing, or who are forced through trafficking into degrading work like prostitution, are likely to feel humiliated as a group but also at a personal level. Such humiliation may never manifest itself in a public way – there may be little chance to do this without reprisal. In other situations humiliation can fuel feelings of grievance at a very basic level and, if other circumstances are present, result in violent retaliation in subsequent generations.

104 Like poverty and inequality, feelings of humiliation can be eased and sometimes even healed over time. None of these things is immutable. One of the ways this has historically happened in the case of humiliation is through programmes of 'reconciliation' and inclusion after prolonged periods of conflict. This is discussed below in the context of breaking down historical narratives of grievance and rebuilding relationships on a different footing.

4. History, Grievance and Conflict

History and grievance are often intertwined

105 Remembered injustices, including those that occurred decades, even centuries before, play an important role in justifying and sustaining many conflicts. Certain remembered processes, the most obvious being colonialism, slavery and the Holocaust, leave a backlog of potentially flammable grievances. Feelings of grievance around a sense of historical injustice need to be understood, not in the sense of what actually happened (this is always open to interpretation) but in terms of what they mean today. However long ago events occurred, it is their interpretation in the light of current circumstances that gives them relevance. These form a backdrop against which more immediate grievances become significant.

106 There are various examples of historic, retained grievance that shape the way in which potential conflict can be kept alive. The Commission observed that the nineteenth-century Irish Famine not only represented massive deprivation and hardship, but also led to deep-seated feelings of anger and disrespect that continue to live on in the minds of later generations that cannot have been directly affected (and sometimes more strongly in the diaspora than in those left behind).

107 In the context of peace and power-sharing in Northern Ireland today, wise and perceptive policy has been aided by an appreciation of, and sensitivity towards, persisting, subliminal grievances on all sides of the traditional fault-line of faith. The recollection of a past

event as divisive as the Battle of the Boyne has been remembered in a way that, since the division of the island, has 'justified' enmity between the two sides.

108 Current leaders have been alive to the need not only to build new political structures but also to address and combat this kind of justification. Failure to do so, they have concluded, would result in a peace that was, and could only ever be, skin deep. What was required, by contrast, is something more ambitious that recognizes the layered and uncritical way in which past grievance has been left to fester and potentially fuel enmity today.

Narratives of grievance can be pervasive

109 How the story of grievance is told to one's own children, community and to others, how it is then reproduced in the media and often, eventually, in school textbooks (thereby institutionalizing it for generations of young people) is an important element in the maintenance and even escalation of disputes, including violent ones.

110 Such narratives bind a community together and unite them around a common cause and this can be positive. But it can also result in portraying the 'other' in a wholly negative light, divesting them of any moral authority or legitimacy; make feelings of hate and distrust 'normal'; and, in extreme cases, be used to justify violence. That is why it is important to nurture across all groups within society a sense of shared common destiny that can transcend long-felt grievances and humiliations.

111 It has been the particular narratives created around shared Muslim global grievance that have been among the most powerful in recent years. Muslims continue to suffer, these narratives will say, simply because the world does not care, or because powerful non-Muslims, especially in the West, feel hatred of Muslims or contempt for Islam. This is a powerful narrative with considerable potential to mobilize opinion in a wide range of similar and dissimilar countries. It is also a narrative that can and has been underscored by attachment to the Muslim Ummah or sense of religious community and common purpose.

112 Sometimes narratives of grievance continue even after peace breaks out. In some cases, it may be that grassroots combatants feel undermined by the peace agreements made in their name – this was the reaction of some loyalist paramilitary groups in Northern Ireland to the Good Friday Agreement. Those involved in gangs or paramilitary groups may also have personal reasons for continuing to fight – it may afford them status amongst their peers or they may be making a living from the violence. Others may always have been involved in violence, since childhood, and never have had the opportunity to stand back and re-think the history of the conflict from their own perspective, but also from the perspectives of others.

113 Importantly, and as we have noted, in order to understand and respect others it is first necessary to be understood and respected oneself.

Reconciliation, often led by women, is a key to healing

114 When conflict ends and reconciliation begins, history needs to be revisited and reinterpreted so that people can move on. Ties that joined the two communities in the past need to be re-emphasized so that scant memories about what times used to be like can be re-ignited. If there was no previous contact, then the affinities they currently share (loyalty to a region, aspects of culture or language) need to be emphasized. Both women and civil society groups have played enormously important roles in reconciliation and peace-building and it is worth considering why their contributions are so significant.

115 Whether women were involved as combatants or not, they are likely to share aspects of their identity and their experience of warfare with women on the 'other' side. Like men, women know what it means to have sons, brothers, husbands and even mothers and daughters, who fought and died in conflict; like men, they know what it means to be displaced. But they are more likely to suffer high rates of maternal and child mortality and low rates of access to

education and health care and to experience exclusion from public life, and they will more often know what it is not to be recognized as full citizens. Women who have survived wars must find ways to live with the gross injustices that have filled their past and are haunting their present – acts of discrimination and violence committed before, during and even after conflict.

116 It is their common experience as women that makes women's role in peace-building so critical, a role that is now formally recognized in UN Security Council Resolution 1325. This resolution attempts to develop a more systematic way of consulting with and involving women in peace and reconstruction processes. The Commission recognizes this crucial role of women, in the hope that their experiences, priorities and solutions contribute more than they have before towards the reconstruction of societies based on inclusive governance. Women can bring some particular strengths and perspectives. For example the fruits of their experience in relating through networks of relationships rather than hierarchical structures is especially important given what we have said earlier about the role of networking in 'government through respectful dialogue'.

117 In Rwanda for example, Tutsi and Hutu widows first came together to take care of war orphans, and are now supporting them by selling their woven baskets in the global market. Women ex-combatants, with first-hand experience as both perpetrators and victims of violence, met to share their experiences and learn ways to manage trauma, and a few have become trainers in the Demobilization and Reintegration Commission, ensuring attention to women's needs in disarmament, demobilization and reintegration. Most notably, by ensuring the inclusion of a 30 per cent quota for women in parliament in the new Constitution, Rwandan women ultimately won a full 49 per cent share – the highest in the world.[1] In Burundi, women from each of the 19 parties to the Arusha peace negotiations came together in the All Party Burundi Women's Peace Conference in July 2000 to formulate an agenda for peace and reconstruction that would guarantee women's rights to rebuild their society alongside men, thereby positioning themselves to enter the political process.[2]

---

1 UNIFEM, 2004-05 and UNIFEM, 2006-07.
2 UNIFEM, 2000.

And through the International Women's Commission for a Just and Sustainable Palestinian–Israeli Peace, prominent Palestinian and Israeli women have come together to advance the peace process and speak with one voice to global leaders.

118 It is instructive to look at how India has opened up the panchayat system, enabling women to take on leadership positions at the local level. Many of these women, nearly 1 million, have been trained in how to analyse local budgets from a gender perspective, making the link between national gender equality policies and actual spending to implement these policies. By looking at budget expenditures, community members are able to ensure that a greater percentage of local resources are spent to provide clean water, health clinics or better local transport systems. They have also engaged in social audits, demanding public review of income and expenditure of village councils and holding officials accountable for addressing, or failing to address, local needs. The positive results of these initiatives show the importance of building women's agency from the bottom up.

119 The role of civil society in post-conflict situations is important for the same reason: civil society groups and organizations can bring together people on the basis of identities they share, not those that have previously divided them. When people meet, for example, as journalists, business people, educationalists or trade union members, and when they are drawn from both sides of previous divisions, they not only bring with them a ready-made network of contacts but also a means of communicating with those contacts. They then have within their grasp the possibility of generating new, jointly developed messages about new ways of relating to each other and working together.

120 The rehabilitation of young people in the immediate aftermath of severe conflict is one of the most challenging tasks facing civil society organizations. We are just beginning to understand the profoundly damaging effects on the personalities of young people who grow up in conflict-ridden societies. Often in the aftermath they find it difficult to live in a peaceful society and have stable personal relationships, and the rate of youth suicides may increase significantly. Where child soldiers have been part of the landscape

of violent conflict, this task can appear daunting given the way in which violence has been habitually embedded in young, formative minds. One programme that has worked in Liberia promotes amputees who have lost limbs in the conflict to take up competitive soccer. People who had been on opposite sides of the fourteen-year conflict in Liberia now play soccer together, often in the same team. The team members themselves see playing soccer together as a great expression of reconciliation.

121   Another important group of people in post-conflict situations are those previously involved in the fighting, including those who have themselves committed atrocities. Very few ex-combatants are given the chance to be listened to and to put their point of view to the wider world. And yet this was a major achievement of South Africa's Truth and Reconciliation Commission, an approach that has since been emulated in many other countries (and had also been used earlier in a number of other countries, particularly in Latin America).

122   The Truth and Reconciliation Commission (TRC) was established in South Africa in 1995 in order to start healing some of the deep wounds of the Apartheid years. The main vehicle of the TRC for this purpose was public storytelling, the aim being to establish a picture of the causes, nature and extent of the violations that had occurred during the Apartheid period. This included both the perspectives of the victims and the motives and perspectives of those responsible for the violations. Amnesty was granted to everyone who fully disclosed what had gone on and this apparently helped enormously in restoring the human dignity of the victims.

123   The TRC thus allowed individuals to tell their story from their own point of view, and to be heard. This proved a major step in the reconciliation process. But it is important to emphasize that its success depended in large part on the fact that it was not – and did not seek to be – a process of redress, and that it was constructed in a particular historic and socio-cultural context.[3] While the exact process cannot simply be repeated in precisely the same way elsewhere, there are important general lessons here on the use of constructive interaction that is an integral part of the civil route to peace.

---

3 Mani, 2002.

5. Political Participation

Dialogue and inclusion

124 In the previous four chapters, this report outlined some of the reasons why respect and understanding are so important at the present time, and the relevance of the Commonwealth approach in engendering a sense of these basic values. It also discussed some of the conceptual issues that underlie violence and concluded that a deeper analysis of these should first inform public debate, and only then feed in to the development of new policies or actions.

125 This chapter begins with an analysis of the constraints that all countries face in ensuring the whole of their population – not just elites and holders of public office – feel fully involved in what has been termed 'government by discussion'. This is about more than putting the right political processes in place, it is also about how these processes are facilitated so that they are truly inclusive – it is the 'how' of political behaviour, not just the 'what'.

126 Furthermore, ways of engendering a sense of belonging, particularly for groups that are traditionally excluded from politics, are discussed. The chapter also considers how political participation might be broadened and extended in situations of peace as well as in post-conflict situations. Going beyond this analysis, therefore, the chapter begins to look at public policy and the messages for governments and civil society. This dual focus – on both substantive analysis and policy messages – is also reflected in future chapters.

An emphasis on the 'how' of political participation

127   A sense of exclusion can arise even in well-established, participatory democratic systems. This is because political inclusion is not only about the form that political systems take (for example, the type of electoral system), but, just as importantly, about how political participation is facilitated throughout the political cycle (and not just at elections). Thus, how debate is managed in local and national political forums, including parliament itself, will reflect on the extent to which the rules of engagement, written or unwritten, provide a containing environment for expression of conflict. It will also be reflected in a context that does, or does not, also allow members to express their strong concerns and feel that they have been listened to – and thus accorded respect.

128   Different perceptions co-exist about the role of opposition parties. Whilst some act primarily as though they are the party in waiting, and therefore spend time consolidating their power base, others focus on the real job of opposition. This is to hold the government of the day to account by listening to the experience of their constituents and being sufficiently well-informed by evidence and argument to support or question the impact of current or planned public policies. Again, the latter approach will make people feel represented and included; the former, typically, will not. The representative duties of parliamentarians are obviously of great importance for the functioning of a civil approach to peace and the avoidance of extremism.

129   Apart from the workings of parliaments, other aspects of democratic systems are also important if 'government by discussion' is to have real meaning. For example, it is critical that people who purport to represent different factions, including parties in conflict, really are representative in a meaningful way, and have representative views that can be attributed to their supporters. All too often, debate can be taken over, or misappropriated, by vocal and more extreme members of a group. These people may not have the actual standing or authority they claim to have; yet their tendency to grab the headlines with inflammatory remarks tends to be seized upon by the media. The perceptions of the general community are then

skewed into believing that all members of the group agree with these inflammatory and disturbing statements.

130 Seeking out those who do in fact represent the group, and do so in a balanced and good-tempered way, is essential and it is a delicate task for government and civil society. The calmer, yet more authentic, leaders and would-be leaders within communities may be repelled by polemic and aggressive behaviour and language. They may, therefore, quite rationally opt not to participate because of the tone, the nature of the discussion, and the manner with which their case is (supposedly) being put. Extremists may also be more likely to be heard if the government does not adequately heed parliament and other legitimate or reasonable representatives.

Communication and consultation styles matter

131 Styles of communication and consultation are particularly important for the participation of women and young people. If serious, experienced and well-intentioned people, with a strong sense of the common good, leave the discussion or never join it, this creates an opportunity for others who may have narrower self-seeking interests to step into the void.

132 In many countries, women are given limited opportunities to develop their skills in participative debate and decision-making at local or national level. In such circumstances, they cannot and do not contribute as equal partners to debates on the development of their communities or countries. One constraint is the absence of laws on gender equality broadly based on international human rights standards. However, the norms of patriarchy and generations of past practice also determine the extent of women's participation in politics at all levels.

133 Nevertheless, it is important to underline that there has been accelerating change in many parts of the Commonwealth on women's participation at the highest levels. The development over many years of a strong female presence in the legal system, in general, and the judiciary, in particular, has led to the appointment this year of the first woman Chief Justice in Ghana, Justice Georgina Woode. These

examples of public commitment to make constructive use of women's agency going well beyond the concern with women's well-being reflect the development over many years, under many governments, of a continuing concern to make an increasingly equal place for women in the legal profession. This is a development that increases the sense among all women that the law need not be blind to women's concerns, but in addition allows the gains from women's active agency to be utilized in the legal systems of these countries. The leadership, for example, of Judge Kate O'Regan on human rights legislation in the South African constitutional court, has greatly assisted the reach of the legal system in this newly democratic country.

134 Elsewhere, in Afghanistan, women participated in the Constitutional *Loya Jirga*[1] (Grand Assembly) elections in June 2002 and in drafting the new Constitution in 2004, and they stood as candidates in the parliamentary and provincial elections of 2005. With help from UN agencies (UNIFEM[2] and UNDP[3]), the women's participation project has also resulted in the adoption of a Constitution with strong provisions for gender equality, including a 25 per cent quota for women in the national and provincial assemblies (which has been achieved), and the formation of a women's caucus in parliament. Although the rise of insurgency, especially in rural areas, threatens these gains, a great deal has been achieved in women's participation in politics since the fall of the Taliban in 2001.

135 And, to offer one final example, Commonwealth countries in South Asia have a lesson to teach others – that is: that women can reach the pinnacle of power. In Sri Lanka, Sirimavo Bandaranaike became Prime Minister in 1959. Her religious background was Buddhism. Indira Gandhi was elected more than once as the Head of the Indian Government. Benazir Bhutto became the first woman Prime Minister of her country, Pakistan, as the Muslim world's first female Head of Government. Bangladesh has produced more than one female political leader in Begum Khaleda Zia and Sheikh Hasina.

---

1 Loya Jirgas (Grand Assemblies) are called in Afghanistan irregularly, often by the ruler. They are attended by tribal/regional leaders, political, military and religious figures, royalty, government officials, etc. The meeting has no time limit, it continues until decisions are reached by consensus on the matter at hand.
2 United Nations Development Fund for Women.
3 United Nations Development Programme.

Young people's involvement requires nurturing

136 Many countries have mechanisms for consulting young people on political issues – for example, via dedicated surveys and more qualitatively by contacting young people's organizations and/or using research teams or interviewers to organize young people into focus groups in order to ascertain their views on a particular subject.

137 But very often this only goes so far; older, more established voices then take over to decide the public policy implications. This is particularly the case in contexts where relations of patriarchy and deference are strong. Young people do need positive role models in authority. But, crucially, they also need spaces in which to build their own confidence and capabilities and have their views taken into account.

138 Authority needs to be exercised in a way that does not end up marginalizing the young and others with little formal voice.

139 Young people therefore emerge as an entry-point for political participation but also as an interest group and a vital resource. They have much more of a sense of the way the world is developing than the current generation of elders. We not only need young people in our families to show us how to work our new machines, we need them to help us design and work our new machinery of governance, and they need the opportunity to work together with groups of older people, as well as independently, to identify innovative ways of tackling deep-seated misconceptions and prejudices, first within their own age group, and then beyond it. There is something of an inter-generational division of labour to aim for:

'We need younger Community leaders to be enthusiastic and give a lead in drawing our communities together. Older people can suggest ways and means by which this can be achieved – but it is the up-and-coming generation of political, civil and religious leaders who need to take up the cause of mutual respect and understanding. For this, they will need training, but above all, enthusiasm, dedication and motivation'.[4]

---

4 Gregorios, 2007.

And civil society has an active role to play

140 In our striving for more liberal democratic societies we have perhaps focused too much on the sporadic involvement given by elections as the solution to the problem of involvement. A society based on 'government by discussion' requires a strong civil society that plays an active role in political debate. Civil society is, of course, very diverse and civil society groups have a range of functions, not all of which are aimed at increasing political voice.

141 Nonetheless research has shown that the 'empowered' citizen emerges gradually, often through local-level debates around jobs, housing or other tangible issues, and only later (sometimes a generation later) gains the independence and knowledge to engage with higher level state processes. Civil society organizations, even if they are not overtly political, can therefore provide the building blocks with which their members may engage with political processes in future, should they wish to.

142 One striking example of this is the role that grassroots organizations played in combating the spread of HIV/AIDS in Australia in the early 1980s. It was at this time that Australia experienced a rapid increase in the incidence of HIV. Peaking in 1984, incidence rates then began to fall dramatically until around 1988.

143 For a long time, the success of early containment had been credited to national initiatives. Recent analysis,[5] however, has shown that these initiatives – the establishment of research institutions, the provision of HIV testing and anti-retroviral drugs, all supported by significant government funding – all came after the decline in incidence rates had begun.

144 Well-organized grassroots activities and structures, by comparison, were in place by 1985. AIDS Action Committees (AACs) were created in major state capitals, the first as early as 1983. The first community-based organization to create a dedicated office in the non-governmental AIDS sector was in place by 1984. And during this time, the medical profession began to rely on the Gay Health Update produced by the Victorian AIDS Council for information on

---

5 Plummer and Irwin, 2006.

how the epidemic was developing. Early reports in the press, the provision of clinical services and community activism all played a key role in Australia's success in combating the spread of HIV/AIDS.

145 Without government initiatives, the decline may not have lasted. This much is clear. But what the research does point to is the ability of community-based and non-governmental organizations to be pro-active; to successfully mobilize communities to provide early intervention and prevention. Governments should seek out organizations with this ability, and help them to build their capacity in a spirit of partnership.

Engendering a sense of belonging

146 For any society to create a common vision for itself, it is necessary for it to find effective ways to nurture a sense of belonging among all its members, including young people. These members are not merely required to be of that society, they are also entitled to be treated in a way that values them as integral to the society. They need to have a sense of being part of a common destiny and a shared future. For this reason alone, there has to be some public endorsement and acceptance of identity even if there are plural identities involved. As mentioned previously, it is preferable for richly textured and multi-layered identities not to be collapsed simplistically into identification based on a single characteristic only, be that racial, linguistic or religious.

147 A traditional liberal and democratic understanding of societal membership has in the past tended to focus on recognition of individuals as citizens. The concept of citizenship is indifferent to group identity or identities – the idea of citizenship does not differentiate or discriminate between people with different identities, it looks at national belonging alone. Identity based on citizenship can amount to an essential lubricant of common belonging and inclusion to work. The idea of national citizenship may be more important for certain groups than others, and may matter in differing ways from one group or context to another.

148 Faith-based organizations have a potentially crucial role and can do much to overcome the constraints that those in the political system may experience. In particular, faith bodies that develop strong bonding relationships among their own members can be in a better position to encourage bridging relationships with those of other faith-identity communities. This can lead to a stronger articulation by faith communities in general of faith and spiritual-oriented approaches to tackling social problems. The role of spirituality in better understanding and responding to the causes of religious extremism and violence is a potentially rich terrain that requires space for consideration.[6]

149 The task is to build the foundations of a community that is both cohesive as well as diverse in its composition. This involves several elements whereby:[7]

- There is a common vision and all communities have a sense of belonging.
- The diversity of people's different backgrounds and circumstances is appreciated and positively valued.
- Those from different backgrounds have similar opportunities. Language fluency and language barriers to entry into particular occupational categories are a prime example that can prevent this.
- Those from different backgrounds develop strong, positive relationships in the workplace, in schools and within neighbourhoods.

Confidence-building in conflict situations carries additional risks

150 Some very specific issues exist around dialogue in conflict situations, particularly when there has been outside military intervention. Even if military intervention is sanctioned by the United Nations, it does not mean that a UN force will be automatically welcomed or their presence accepted by local populations. Whether this happens will depend in large part on how the intervention is managed

6 Taylor, 2007.
7 Malik, 2005.

and how processes for dialogue with local leaders and people are developed. This involves literally how the actions of those on the ground are able to gain, or do not gain, the confidence of people and institutions. However bad the situation that led to the intervention, no occupying force can expect local support unless people themselves feel included and respected.

Commonwealth principles in action

151 The Commonwealth is sometimes criticized for talking first, often, and for a very long time on an issue of contention without reaching any resolution. But this report of the Commission endorses this approach as an essential way of dealing with problems of respect and understanding – as well as a way to reduce violence and the incidence and impact of terrorism.

152 Criticism of the Commonwealth approach fails to acknowledge that:

- The practical application of Commonwealth principles has yielded significant change in some of the largest conflicts of the contemporary world, such as South Africa.
- Practitioners of these principles have gained currency for their style of engagement that respects differences of identity and viewpoint.
- These principles place leaders in a strong and credible position in searching for the underlying causes of conflict and violence.
- The Commonwealth approach has fresh relevance as the reputation of more confrontationist approaches has begun to falter.

153 Talking alone cannot solve all the world's problems. It is doubtful what could have been achieved by talking for longer in Afghanistan, Yugoslavia or Rwanda as the events that occurred in all these places were not obviously due to a lack of dialogue but for other reasons. Sometimes conflict can escalate to extreme levels of violence so quickly (as in Rwanda) that face-to-face discussion is hard to achieve. But problems in Northern Ireland were resolved by talking, India and Pakistan are talking rather than going to war, and it is not beyond

the bounds of possibility to believe that in the end relations between Israel and Palestine may yet be resolved through a long-term process of dialogue and deeper mutual respect and understanding.

Promoting democracy through institutional best practice

154 The Commonwealth is currently engaged in a wide range of activities designed to ensure adherence to best practice in democratic political participation. One example is the role of election observers – widely accepted as a mean to ensure that the processes of elections are fair and unbiased. This kind of intervention is especially valuable where recent past experience has meant that there is little public confidence in the democratic electoral process itself.

155 Election observation is an example of confidence building in that it is designed to deter the use of domineering or oppressive behaviour by particular groups, through independent documentation of the election process by third parties. Independence lies at its heart, indeed, the Commonwealth 'brand' is widely trusted perhaps more than any other. The Commonwealth offers election observation only when invited and so all parties have an incentive to comply with international standards and a reason to accept the observers' judgments.

156 There is a rub, however, namely that election observation is an intervention that comes late in the process and inevitably avoids looking at behaviour and standards beforehand. A more holistic picture reveals that intimidation, exclusion and other indirect threats to general public confidence may be present a long time before an election is staged. The problem, therefore, largely occurs further upstream and needs to be tackled at that earlier point.

157 Limiting these influences may be laudable during an election process, but the problems may have set in well before the election campaign begins. There can be longstanding negative attitudes, practices and behaviour which become more plainly expressed during an election process. There is, therefore, a strong case to look at:

- how interventions to promote democratic engagement might be used in the period between election campaigns; and

- how to grow the capacity of local institutions and groups as buttresses for democracy.

158 The latter include genuinely independent electoral commissions to oversee behaviour and adherence to fair processes including funding arrangements for parties and candidates, parliamentary secretariats to support the scrutiny functions of parliamentarians, and finally technical assistance to election observer missions that train and support good practice among local election officials.

159 A bigger challenge even than this lies in finding new ways to promote legitimate and credible interaction between governments and oppositions after the elections in different Commonwealth countries. In circumstances where electoral systems are based on a single majority-simple plurality (SMSP) principle, the outcome can often be a winner-takes-all situation triggered by being the first-past-the-post. Holding a monopoly of executive power carries with it serious consequences and risks. Chief among these is the on-going need to involve and retain the confidence of opposition parties and candidates who do not participate in government.

160 Opposition involvement and buy-in to the process is valuable yet often elusive. Specifically, their involvement is critical to sustain backing for the legitimacy of the political system as opposed to the government of the day. In other words, the task is to strike a balance: to nurture backing for the office of government whilst remaining agnostic towards the office-holder.

161 Executive dominance of this kind is a direct cause for concern in itself. But it is particularly dangerous if it is in the hands of a particular ethnic or religious group, perhaps via a party system that is built around ethno-religious lines. Interventions to help broaden out 'government by discussion' in systems where power is concentrated in the hands of the executive can be pursued in various ways. For leaders, such broadening can happen in three main ways, (these strategies are not mutually exclusive but each involves a particular area of concentration). They can:

- try to dilute the executive monopoly of power by building in some element of power sharing;

- strengthen the balancing role of parliament and the judiciary; and
- support media, civil society and community-based efforts to demand greater accountability.

162 Building in an element of power sharing to the executive has been addressed, for instance by establishing extra-parliamentary forums in which government–opposition interaction is routinized, and where complex issues to do with public confidence in the democratic process are aired. The Commonwealth's Good Offices work has sought to further this kind of assistance. The Commonwealth Ministerial Action Group acts as a guardian of the fundamental principles of the Commonwealth. It is also possible for Commonwealth countries to turn to other Commonwealth states for expert assistance and advice, as the UK did from time to time in the Northern Ireland process.

6. The Role of the Media and Communication

Media messages convey important influences

163 Mass media and other forms of communication technology have an enormous influence in helping to shape public opinion and underlying sentiment. Newspapers, TV and radio are all important sources of basic information about other people and other places and this can itself help to engender understanding if presented in a fair, even-handed and non-inflammatory way.

164 The media is also an important accountability mechanism: it raises important issues, corruption for example, that might otherwise never be publicly debated or addressed. The media also has an important role in stimulating governments to take action on social policy: although stories about migrants or refugees might reinforce prejudice in some quarters, they also expose problems that need to be addressed, for example poor living conditions or lack of access to services, the citizenship status of migrants, the response of local communities to their settlement and so on.

165 But the media can also, in some cases, become an instrument for the dissemination of false and inflammatory messages and values that do not promote respect or well-tempered dialogue and discussion. Negative messages can divide communities and can help perpetuate the stereotypes that nurture violence.

166 Media portrayals can sometimes serve to exacerbate the narrative of oppositional forces and irreconcilable, value-based differences. The media often prefers to dwell on conflict, since conflict and drama

sell newspapers and attract an audience. This inevitably means that the more extreme points of view get airtime rather than the feelings of the majority of citizens that may have more accommodating and balanced perspectives. For example, during the 1994 Rwandan genocide, the state-supported Radio Télévision Libre des Mille Collines (RTLM) station broadcast hate propaganda against Tutsis, moderate Hutus, Belgians and the United Nations, and was used as a tool to organize massacres. And even when the media are truly independent, there can be a tendency by some (though not all) of the media to oversimplify the complexity of current problems and reduce the news to catch phrases and sound bytes – on the assumption that people want drama and entertainment rather than informed analysis. An emphasis on the constructive role of the media, which we strongly support, has to go with a realistic recognition of the problems that the media have reason to guard against.

And new media serve to shape outlooks more directly

167 The internet has radically changed the way in which people communicate and connect with each other. As a means of social interaction, the web brings people together – friends, family, young people, or complete strangers that share interests or objectives – and this can foster a sense of belonging and identity. The web, however, has also been used to target people, mainly young users, to radicalize them into specific belief systems and divisive ways of seeing the world.

168 Some constructive means of linking like-minded peaceful groups across dispersed regions already exists – including those such as 'Youth for a Sustainable Future', an email discussion group founded by young people in the Pacific to discuss issues affecting themselves and the region.

169 However, the riots in Cronulla, in southern Sydney, Australia, in December 2005 are an interesting illustration of the role of the media and modern forms of communication like text messaging

in a less peaceful direction. For some time, there had been a growing escalation of hostilities between some members of the local Anglo-Australian community and Middle Eastern people at Cronulla Beach. Over a 36-hour period there was a rapid build-up of violence, and a reaction 24 hours later by those who had been subjected to violence, to a great extent using organized text messaging.

170 Cronulla Beach became the contested space between people of Middle Eastern background on the one hand and the 'traditional' Anglo-Australians for whom Cronulla was the home of their traditional surf beach culture. In the weeks leading up to the conflict, the media reported stories of beachgoers who complained that they had had sand flicked in their faces by young men of Middle Eastern background while they were playing soccer, and there were other reports of Middle Eastern men who made offensive remarks about women who were wearing bikinis and other clothes that the men considered immodest and offensive. The conflict escalated one Saturday afternoon in early December 2005, stoked by a huge proliferation by white youths of text messaging up and down the coastal beaches of Sydney.

171 On a more positive note, the riots caused a great deal of reflection about the nature and impact of some media coverage, and soul searching about how to mitigate a sense of exclusion and hostility by some groups. Surf lifesaving clubs, the bastion of surf and local community culture, have been opened up to members of different groups. There has been a successful programme to encourage young Muslim people to train as lifesavers, and modesty-driven adaptations to traditional women's swimming costumes have been designed for young Muslim women who want to enjoy the beach and participate in community activities.

172 Sometimes the internet has been used for fomenting group violence. Taking the rough with the smooth, an awareness of this problem is important, while building on the constructive role of the media and public dialogue.

The media can have innovative roles in breaking down conflict

173 Other media initiatives have been successful at increasing the inclusion of previously marginalized groups by providing them with a means of expressing their views. Positive results have also resulted from the creation of channels through which older, familiar binary disputes can be broken down and re-imagined in ways that highlight common interests that transcend warring boundaries.

174 In the occupied Palestinian territory, an on-going Palestinian initiative aims to promote gender equity through media capacity-building and outreach. The programme created networks of local media professionals (male and female) in the different communities, trained them to produce, print and broadcast programmes on women's lives and issues, and fostered relationships, collaboration and information-sharing between women leaders and media professionals. Training was provided to women leaders in media presentation skills, and to public information officers in media advocacy campaigns. As a result, several long-term relationships were established between women's organizations and television and radio stations, enabling women to continue sharing information and informing broadcasts. This initiative for the Promotion of Global Dialogue and Democracy (MIFTAH) is supported by UNIFEM.

175 Another interesting example of a direct effort to promote goodwill between nations was the US government's sponsorship of the band Audioslave on a tour of Cuba. In what seemed to be a sort of peace offering, few were able to discern exactly what the US government was trying to achieve, or what the Cuban government was receiving in return. The spectacle of Audioslave trying to 'make friends' with Cuba with the endorsement of the US government, in a way that US foreign policy had failed to achieve over almost half a century, is a powerful reminder of the influence of music.

176 The world of journalism has also grasped opportunities to promote understanding in conflict situations. In Northern Ireland, just before the Good Friday Agreement, the editors of a Catholic nationalist newspaper and a Protestant unionist newspaper developed a joint initiative. They asked their readers to 'Call this number if you say

"Yes to Peace"'. The fact that the two main newspapers on opposite sides of the divide ran the same text with the same notice was very powerful. A total of 145,000 calls were made, and with a local population of only 1.5 million people, this amounted to a significant one-in-ten response rate.

177 This initial success led to another interesting venture where each editor wrote an editorial in favour of peace for the same day, and sent it to each other in advance, working on the drafts until they had a single editorial to which they could both sign up. As a result, Protestants and Catholics in Northern Ireland could read the same words in 'their' separate newspapers, and know that the editors they trusted had been able to express the same sentiments, while remaining true to their interests. It was a powerful piece of innovative journalism and became something of a story in itself.

178 A broader task, jointly faced by Commonwealth members and media professionals, is to develop a more critical understanding of international issues. The UN Alliance of Civilizations report highlighted this area for special concern, and noted that taking corrective measures would greatly help to inform publics in various countries in a balanced way about international issues. Professional schools of journalism and media are particularly important in achieving this kind of wider orientation of the role of journalists and other media professionals. Media responsibility is the ethical correlative of media freedom.

7. Young People and Education

Young people and the respect and understanding agenda

179 More than 60 per cent of the Commonwealth's population are aged under 30 years; the proportion is closer to three-quarters in some member countries. Young people are the inheritors of a changing world – its economic distributions, social positions, cultural identities and historical narratives. They need not be passive recipients of these things; with appropriate support and political will young people can be an active, positive force for development, locally, nationally and internationally.

180 But for this to happen, they need to be seen and treated as potential assets and engaged in processes of dialogue and decision-making. They need to be included in forums where it is possible to listen and participate, but also to put forward their own point of view and have their own narratives heard, discussed and debated. There also needs to be a deeper understanding of the inter-generational transmission of narratives.

181 In this regard, we have to recognize the critical importance of school principals and administrators – and eventually teachers – as leaders who can potentially change social reality by the way in which they manage their schools. Schools, after all, often have diverse workforces themselves (that is, teachers) and the principal can set the tone for the entire school and thereby influence the way in which the children grow up thinking about issues such as community, religion and violence.

182 Most young people enter workforces that have either a limited demand for their skills or where there are very few opportunities

for decent work at all. Between 2000 and 2015 an estimated 1 billion young men and women will enter the labour market and try to find work – but there will not be 1 billion jobs waiting for them. In terms of both the uncertainty of employment and the fact that as young people they are simply not accorded respect in many societies, they are in some senses a marginalized group. But they are also unlikely to self-identify as a group, still less to organize as a social force.

183   The Commission notes that it is essential to think about respect and understanding in an inter-generational context, and to be acutely aware of the impact of societal norms, particularly patriarchy and deference, on the self-confidence and development of young people. In many situations, authority structures need to be reconstructed so they do not silence young people, and particularly young women and other groups whose voice is normally stilled through a reference to 'tradition' or 'custom'.

184   When young people are disenfranchised or humiliated or made to feel that they have little say and no future, they may become drawn into movements or ideologies that appear to guarantee them a place in the world and give them a solid identity. In some instances, inspiring or forceful leaders may draw them into conflicts as combatants, literally as foot soldiers. World-wide an estimated 300,000 people under the age of 18 are now, or have recently been, involved in armed conflict, and another 500,000 have been recruited into military or paramilitary forces.

185   But young people need not be only the victims or perpetrators of violence; they also have an important role as peace-makers. They are not so much the problem as at the heart of the solution.

186   Some of the most innovative programmes for involving young people in post-conflict reconstruction are provided by Commonwealth programmes themselves – an example is the project that explicitly seems to build respect and understanding among and between former child soldiers, young people and adults in the former conflict zone of Northern Uganda.

187   More generally, Commonwealth programmes provide examples of how young people's presence and skills can be valued, appreciated and used in activities normally undertaken only by adults. The

Commonwealth Youth Programme engages young people in its own governance structures whilst youth representatives are included as members of election observation missions.

188 Other programmes focus on working alongside stigmatized groups. Groups in society with illnesses or diseases that are seen as a social taboo are often at the harsh end of casual, and sometimes even official, vilification and hatred. Their treatment amounts to an especially offensive form of disrespect, particularly if their original ailment or suffering is the product of poverty, hardship and ignorance.

Youth Ambassadors for Positive Living

189 Respect and understanding for people living with AIDS is promoted through a 'Youth Ambassadors for Positive Living' programme, operating in Africa, Asia and the Caribbean. The Youth Ambassadors are usually HIV-positive volunteers who engage in peer education and campaign for appropriate policy responses among government and civil society. Their message is one of de-stigmatization.

190 One of the future activities planned is to develop learning materials for political literacy. The aim would be to enhance the capacity of organized youth groups and others to become effective advocates for democracy and good governance through their participation in observer missions, peace-building initiatives and other governance processes. This is very much in the mould of building resilience to extremism.

191 These are just a few of many examples. The challenge is to broaden and extend the effective participation of young women and men in the development process in their own countries and regions.

Empowerment can be created through youth parliaments

192 In the Pan-Commonwealth Youth Caucus, as well as in the overall youth sector in the Pacific Islands region, there is much discussion

surrounding the need for countries to host annual or bi-annual Youth Parliaments to promote good governance through positive practice. Youth Parliaments, of which there are several models throughout the world, are exercises in which young people elect their own leaders and participate in a two-week parliamentary debate on issues of their choosing. The resolutions are then passed on to relevant government departments, the national legislative assembly and donors for consideration and further action.

193 The Tonga Youth Parliament is aiming to promote good governance through a different method in the near future. Rather than only electing young leaders, the Tonga National Youth Congress, with assistance from the Pacific Islands Forum Secretariat (PIFS), will train these leaders to behave with a level of respect appropriate to members of a national legislative assembly. When the young people act in a more respectful way, the expectation is that they will influence not only other young leaders but the national legislative assembly as well. The entire Youth Parliament is televised live and is also aired on the radio throughout all of the islands.

Sport can also promote empowerment and mutual understanding

194 The Commonwealth Games, perhaps one of the most visible and well-known aspects of the Commonwealth, are another good example of how the Commonwealth already promotes respect and understanding. Also known as the 'friendly games', the Games promote the pursuit of health and provide an opportunity for young people to strive for excellence, more so since the inauguration of the four-yearly Commonwealth Youth Games in 2000.

195 Sport is a vocation open to all people, irrespective of disability, ethnicity or economic position. Rigorous training and a commitment to winning medals for one's nation can help to overcome any perceived divides within that nation. The impact of the Games goes beyond the quadrennial event. In its commitment to the three core values of humanity, equality and destiny, the Commonwealth Games Federation also seeks to improve the lives and societies

of Commonwealth people by assisting education through sport development and physical recreation.[1]

Education is inevitably central to the cause of respect and understanding

196 In the longer run, the biggest gains in shaping shared narratives across potential divides will most likely come from investment in, and rethinking of, education. This was one of the most frequently mentioned channels through which respect and understanding could be engendered that was identified by the Commission and by the high-level submissions made to the work of the Commission.

197 Thinking strategically about education, and especially about how to deliver education as a suitable intervention means several different things. It is helpful to break these down:

- Educational participation itself can be an important symptom of embedded inequality and lack of opportunity. The distribution of education shapes tendencies towards inclusion or exclusion and, thus, general patterns that are evident in a particular society. The effects on respect and understanding can be substantial, although they may be indirect in their nature. Policy-makers are faced with the job of developing mechanisms to widen and deepen educational participation as a means of (a) overcoming societal tendencies to exclusion and/or (b) compensating for the injustice and/or barriers experienced by a particular group.
- Extending the age 'reach' of the compulsory schooling system upwards and downwards – and implementing this effectively – is extremely important. So also is extending participation in basic education in rural communities. The use of pioneering programmes to preserve household income generated through informal child working, whilst delivering a core education programme, is another important way of extending educational participation. The 'who' aspects of education are therefore central.

---

1 See www.thecgf.com

- Educational content is linked with the promotion of respect and understanding – or the opposite. Thus the educational curriculum is central in embodying and communicating values and messages about the relationships and understandings between and across existing identity groups. Teaching children in the compulsory schooling system about the cultural heritage of a range of ethnic and religious communities is a typical intervention based on multicultural models of stimulating appetite for knowledge. As well as giving an understanding of comparative religion and ethnic and cultural groups, it is important to teach children that there are fundamental human values that transcend religion, cultural and ethnic boundaries – the duty to treat others with respect and dignity, and to do unto others as you wish to be treated yourself.

198 Knowledge of world history is particularly critical in helping to forge cosmopolitan identities. Equally, teaching children about the value and purpose of social cohesion based on mutual equality is another, rather more ambitious intervention. Finally, teaching can develop a range of ways to transfer knowledge in plural societies. Softer aspects of education are also relevant in relation to smoothing the adaptation of immigrants to their host or new home societies. The 'what' aspects of education are at the heart of all of these interventions.

- Educational contributions to the larger task of managing difference are important. The extent to which education plays a positive role in engendering respect for difference depends on how it is framed and used in a social context. Canadian bi-lingualism policies, for example, seek to go beyond expanding language usage and also offer an alternative way to think about education for all communities, irrespective of their particular identities or lines of heritage. Education in this sense is very much about preparing young – or younger – minds to live in and cope effectively with a world of various pluralisms.

199 Education is also an instrument for understanding both difference and the potential for fault-lines to descend into conflict and violence. At its most effective, education can be used to reflect on and gain a better understanding of conflict itself, insofar as knowledge can be conveyed in a way that shows that every major conflict involves

an interaction between economic, political, historical and cultural factors and that in many cases, group mobilization occurs along lines of ethnic, religious or ideological identity, which destroys ties of respect and understanding and replaces them with fear and mistrust. The 'how' aspects of education's role in shaping much larger social cohesion lie at the heart of this kind of educational approach and one interesting example, in a context where the majority of children are still educated in faith-related schools, is the Northern Ireland Education for Mutual Understanding initiative, which has been incorporated as a curriculum requirement.

200 The question of the renewal of the Commonwealth itself cannot be lightly dismissed in the context of education. Such renewal is possible only when we are able to discover and to keep re-discovering who we really are, how our lives have been forged from that textured history of hundreds of years, of which both the idea of Pax Britannica and the Commonwealth are also products.

201 Education is not just about school and college education, it is about life-long learning, including in very particular situations. Thus, for example, it includes programmes that aim to bring conflicting parties together in peace-building activities or in political education programmes in post-conflict situations.

202 Young people can and do play a role here, including as advisers and trainers. 'Education' also includes providing training support for young people to engage in and participate in governance processes – in youth organizations, trade unions, National Youth Councils and Parliaments. The Commonwealth Youth Programme has a large number of innovative programmes that encourage youth participation in a variety of functions; all seek to both inform and empower young people.

203 The Commission attaches importance to quality, relevant education, regardless of whether that education is provided by the state or not. In many countries, the non-government educational system has increased exponentially in response to lack of government resources to equip and staff government schools adequately (including valuing and remunerating teachers in ways that ensures their attendance). Bangladesh is perhaps one of the most interesting examples of this, with enormous investments by the NGO sector

in children's and adult (particularly women's) education. The role of government then changes to one of providing a policy and regulatory framework, through which it can exert influence over wider educational objectives.

204 The Commission concluded that state policies that actively promote new faith schools, whether they are Christian, Jewish, Muslim or Hindu, may be problematic if the impact of these schools is that students learn to see the world in fragmented terms, with their faith identity setting them apart from others with different faiths or no faith at all. The proliferation of faith schools today comes at a time when prioritizing religion in particular ways has been a major contributory factor to violence in many parts of the world. It is important, therefore, to insist that education is:

'...not just about getting children, even very young ones, immersed in an old, inherited ethos. It is also about helping children to develop the ability to reason about new decisions that any grown-up person will have to take...and enhance (their) capability...to live "examined lives" as they grow up in an integrated country.'[2]

205 Whether faith or secular, public or private, the emphasis must be on providing a high-quality, rounded education that encourages respect between all peoples and does not put forward the idea that any one dogma is pre-eminent. Faith schools are able to deliver this objective, so long as blinkered dogma is not the lens for their students.

206 There is a need for all countries to look at the totality of their education systems, both as sources of current marginalization but also as sources of huge potential to help overcome that marginalization. Education is paramount in the process of promoting respect and understanding between people, and particularly the young – the leaders, followers, thinkers and doers of the future. What they are taught and how they are taught is critical.

207 The Commission emphasizes the critical role of education, defined in its broadest sense, in engendering a feeling of respect and understanding amongst diverse populations and particularly the young. The organizations that deliver these different educational programmes are as simple as school systems and as high-level as Commonwealth forums.

---

2 Sen 2006, 160.

8. Multilateralism and the International Order

A way of thinking and acting

208 The challenges of global violence and hatred are by no means new to governments and the international community. One of the core insights provided by its work is that one-sided imposed solutions have tended to fail in carrying hearts and minds, and that therefore such approaches are unlikely to be effective or credible.

209 The task is to arrive at an approach or style of engagement that is effective and credible precisely because the measures required can be sustained over a long period. Credibility accrues from having to build and nurture coalitions of interest, having to take into account the opinions of others, having to keep open lines of communication, and from affording respect to those of different views and values. The issue of effectiveness requires asking the simple question: does an intervention that is unilaterally imposed actually work in achieving its stated goals?

210 We have focused very heavily in this report on the need for more economically advanced countries to deal respectfully and with understanding in their relationships with other states, but it is important to point out that this is a two-way process. It is also the case that poorer countries must deal fairly with the more economically advanced countries. There are some leaders who dismiss all efforts by new leaders in these economically advanced countries to change and improve relationships. They wish to hold the new generation to account in perpetuity for all the misdeeds of history. Such snubs and rebuffs to those in the less economically

advanced world who do wish to build respect and understanding is likely to be very counter-productive for all concerned. Respect and understanding is a process of mutuality.

211 These then are some of the hallmarks of a positive and constructive multilateral approach. They have substantial value in helping governments and others to address grievance and humiliation in order to curb violence and hatred. The Commonwealth itself is deeply imbued with this approach and its underlying philosophy of engagement. And, indeed, the Commission itself has carried out its task at the behest of a multilateral organization. This necessarily implies a particular way of looking at, and thinking about, problems and arriving at better, shared solutions.

Multilateralism and unilateralism

212 Acting multilaterally has many advantages and these should be recalled at the outset:

- Multilateralism amounts to a way of looking at things in a rounded and balanced manner, with a sensitivity to the true complexities of the international problems faced by countries today.

- More often than not, the international order is more effectively served by, and geared to, this approach than to Big Power politics. Few, if any, powerful countries can act to preserve their interests alone. Even Big Powers implicitly, and explicitly through their membership of international organizations like the UN and Commonwealth and accession to international instruments, accept the case for working with others to secure their own interests and international order.

- The complexity of many current and emerging international issues is suited to a multilateral approach. This is because many of these issues embody the collective interests and responsibilities of all countries or of a group. Examples might be neighbours sharing a common resource or affected by a particular event, or facing a common environmental challenge, or a disparate group with a common interest such as economic vulnerability.

213 The Commission recognizes that there may be situations in which unilateral action may be required and is permissible under international law, for example, self defence or in defence of a nation's citizens. However, even in cases where unilateral intervention has been required, or has taken place, it is striking to observe in many cases that there was a continuing need for multilateral tools to promote dialogue and afford dignity in reaching a solution. The latter may become small yet essential tests of the willingness of the powerful to engage with, and respond positively to, the interests and perspectives of the less powerful. There is a need to find answers which address the concerns and hopes of all parties, and this means that any approach where one side has a 'winner takes all' attitude is unlikely to be credible or effective.

214 The Commonwealth approach of dialogue and consensus building, in which even the least powerful member must be fully consulted, is an important example of this inherently multilateral approach. And as all members use the English language, communication can be both more efficient and more informal. As a result, the Commonwealth can use the power of language as a mechanism for protecting not only civil liberties, but also cultural rights.

215 South Africa stands out as perhaps the most striking example of the Commonwealth approach in action. Even when the country withdrew from the organization in the early 1960s, the Commonwealth, rather than forsaking South Africa, made it a centrepiece of its activity. First it set out the position of principle, clearly defined in the condemnation of Apartheid and racism in the 1971 Singapore Principles. Then it moved to concrete actions such as sporting and economic sanctions, grappling with differences between member states in finding a broadly supported approach. At the same time it pushed the boundaries for engagement, highlighted by the 1985 Eminent Persons Group mission to South Africa. Then in the early 1990s it supported the internal negotiating process which led in 1994 to a free multi-racial South Africa and its return not only to Commonwealth membership, but Commonwealth leadership, with its hosting of the 1999 Durban CHOGM.

216 In the course of this, South Africa itself has become something of a model for a 'rainbow nation', with mechanisms to address past grievance and some of the strongest protections of individual and community rights in the world.

217 More recently, in the last decade in Nigeria and Sierra Leone the Commonwealth rallied round to support the people of these nations as they faced up to military dictatorships. In the case of Sierra Leone, members co-operated with military as well as political support to see the legitimate government of President Kabbah returned. But in both cases, the crucial Commonwealth role came in the peace-building phase which followed democratic elections, when they worked with a wide range of international partners to support these members as they reclaimed civil government and grappled with the roots of past grievances. In both countries the Commonwealth-supported efforts continue.

218 These are familiar and credible examples of the multilateralist approach at work and bringing about concrete results. The outcomes have delivered benefits to all sides. And this is where the approach has direct relevance for today's conflicts. In some countries the approach has yielded greater freedoms for legitimate opposition parties and movements. In others, it has allowed greater inclusion of marginalized groups into the mainstream of society. And in yet others, it has spawned realistic and holistic strategies to combat terror.

219 It is this philosophy which also stands behind the Secretary-General's Good Offices work, to address potential causes of conflict and involve all parties in sustainable political and social solutions. In member nations as diverse as Guyana, Cameroon, Swaziland and Maldives these efforts have had considerable success and have been much appreciated by member governments. The Commission commends these Good Offices activities of the Commonwealth and the philosophy which inspires them as having a wide relevance for addressing grievance internationally, and acting as a model of multilateral support in support of the challenges faced by nations.

Late, though not lost, opportunities

220 It must be acknowledged that this approach, slow and consultative by nature, is not always immediately successful. Zimbabwe, which has withdrawn from the Commonwealth, is a case in point. In Zimbabwe, the absence of a viable political solution acceptable to all sides that also addresses longstanding grievances, as well as a failure to meet Commonwealth concerns and expectations, remains a major concern. But this absence should not be taken to infer that such an outcome cannot yet be attained by the use of a Commonwealth, multilateralist approach. The South African case gives hope for a way forward. By going with the grain of the approach outlined here, the Commission desperately hopes that a successful outcome in Zimbabwe remains within reach. The current situation is a cruel and unnecessary tragedy for the people of Zimbabwe.

221 This approach may also have something to offer in the current vexed context of Iraq, where there are growing calls for greater multilateral engagement. It can be argued that the escalation of violence in Iraq under occupation following recent elections illustrates the penalties of a singular concentration on voting (the illusion that 'if there are elections we have a functioning democracy'), since democratic political processes often require public discussion, including addressing new divisions as well as the history of past tensions and conflicts. There is a great need to ensure a political and security climate in which public discussion without barriers of community divisions can proceed. The international community needs to help promote this public discussion.

222 Afghanistan's difficulties also represent a late, though not lost, opportunity for multilateralism, especially given the political commitment of the United Nations. The Afghan people underwent untold suffering over several decades of armed conflict, which was triggered by the invasion of Afghanistan by foreign troops. The Geneva Accords, signed in 1988, entrusted the UN with a monitoring role and the expectation that Afghanistan would thus be restored to its people, and a multi-ethnic democracy would be set up. This expectation remains unrealized, as externally supported inter-ethnic

conflict prevents the restoration of peace and the return home of large numbers of refugees and displaced persons. Afghanistan has in effect become an abandoned state. The UN Strategic Framework for Afghanistan statement prepared in September 1998 described the desperate reality of Afghanistan thus:

'It mixes a volatile and violent political crisis, a human rights and humanitarian emergency, and two decades of missed development opportunities. The fragmentation of the country and the collapse of practically all institutions of the State, also constitute "an emergency of governance".'[1]

223 The Commission believes that a multilateralist approach remains the most credible way forward. The 2001 Bonn Agreement contained the following core elements of a strategy to rescue and rebuild Afghanistan:

- A process to be nurtured and facilitated by the UN which would involve all segments of the Afghan population and enable them to participate in the implementation of the framework and basis of lasting peace in Afghanistan.
- A process of meaningful consultations to be sustained with all segments of the Afghan people in all parts of Afghanistan and those displaced outside the country.
- The basic elements of the framework were: (a) recognition of the right to choose freely a broad-based, multi-ethnic and fully representative government consisting of representatives of all segments of the Afghan people; (b) an inclusive participatory process which would involve continuing consultations to spell out each phase of the transition and clearly formulated steps to be taken in each phase; (c) while this transition was being affected within the agreed framework, the international community would commit the needed resources to support the process of re-construction and in particular to the strategic goal of building capacity for providing national security.

224 The Commission believes that strong international engagement will continue to be required to address the remaining challenges. Unemployment, the large-scale revival of poppy cultivation, and

---

1 Reproduced in Hossain 1999.

the increasing insurgency of the Taliban are matters of grave concern. Therefore, a meaningful contribution can be made towards truly restoring Afghanistan to all of its peoples. This involves a resumption of the Commonwealth approach by the international community in order to reinstate genuine stability and democracy through development and the participation of people affected by violence and fragmentation. Respect and understanding among all the segments of the Afghan population must provide the foundation for a multi-ethnic and stable democracy.

225 Similar approaches and conclusions can be applied to other outstanding conflicts and trouble-spots within and beyond the Commonwealth:

- Combating extremism and terrorism requires governments to go beyond security and intelligence measures. Sustained solutions are most likely through multilateral co-operation to isolate and deplete support for extremist ideologies of hatred and fear.
- Unilateral military interventions, sometimes guided by humanitarian motives, are nevertheless dependent on securing political settlements rapidly in their wake. Failure to arrive at such a settlement risks returning to earlier cycles of violence and even escalation with greater turmoil and suffering.
- Long-standing opponents have, in some cases, been able to liberate themselves from a winner-takes-all mindset. Multilateralist thinking has been critical in doing so. In Northern Ireland, a peace dividend now combines with a security dividend with benefits for all.

Respect and understanding have to be carried to issues of injustice and the international order

226 At any moment in history, there are grievances that have to do with the perceived unfairness of the world system and the unjustly strident behaviour of powerful countries or blocs. The reasons for sentiments of injustice depend to a great extent on historical circumstance and the balance of power in that particular period – thus grievances experienced by people and countries during the Cold War have different geneses than grievances experienced today.

227 As with local-level conflicts conducted through the lens of identities, there is an initial tendency to explain feelings of global injustice primarily in economic terms. Some have argued that it is the lack of economic integration of Southern economies into the neo-liberal global economic system, which is the cause of social dislocation, and that the economic hegemony of Western countries has provoked Islamic militancy.

228 There is some basic logic in this argument. The extensive restructuring of the world system of production and division of labour during the past 20 years has generated unprecedented benefits for some regions, countries and individuals. However, the effects are highly uneven, including within countries.

229 Poorer countries have borne the brunt of demographic pressures. Migration, predominantly of young people, is one example. It is estimated that in 2005 there were over 191 million international migrants worldwide,[2] the majority from developing countries. This has had a major negative impact on the skills base of developing countries. At the same time, in the receiving countries it tends to increase competition between disadvantaged groups as they struggle for jobs, housing and services. But more positively it has enormously increased the diversity of peoples in developed countries. Furthermore, remittances to developing countries as a result have contributed significantly to their capital inflows and community development. Although the persistence of high levels of poverty and unequal participation in international decision-making processes create a sense of being 'left behind' in the broad sweep of globalisation, there are also other factors operating.

The stark problem of double standards

230 The Commission concludes that a more significant issue – and one of the underlying causes of a deep sense of injustice in the world today – is not the economic hegemony of (largely) Western industrialized nations per se, but rather, the perception that some of these nations have created an environment where there are no rules based on

---

2 UN DESA 2005, 1.

international law, only national self-interest. This, then, plays into the hands of extremist groups with a grievance agenda:

'Organisations that employ terror have gained legitimacy by the often cynical, hypocritical and abusive exercise of power in the international realm by today's most developed democracies. Preaching the protection of rights at home, the military and intelligence organisations of the great powers have too often supported abusive regimes abroad if in doing so they gain strategic military advantage or access to natural resources'.[3]

231 Instances of nations acting in this manner have long historical roots. Throughout the colonial period and during the Cold War, both Western governments and the Soviet Union supported proxy wars in third countries, particularly in Africa, Latin America and South-East Asia. Taking advantage of local grievances and conflict but often funded by outsiders, these wars subverted people's democratic rights and had devastating effects on the lives of all those caught up in them.

232 Although the incidence of proxy wars has decreased since the end of the Cold War, the involvement of rich countries in armed conflicts in third states continues through the export of arms. Of the total exports of conventional arms in the world in 2006, as much as 79 per cent was sold by the five permanent members of the Security Council, and 80 per cent by the G8 countries, with many countries common to both lists.[4]

233 If the average spent on arms every year had been put to the service of education and health in Africa, Asia, the Middle East and Latin America, it is estimated that every child could be in school and child mortality could be reduced by two-thirds – fulfilling two of the MDGs by 2015. Responsibility for the 'opportunity cost' of arms is that of buying countries, but also of the G8 nations.

234 In recent years, the perception of injustice and a failure to protect human rights in the conflict in the Middle East generally, and the Israeli–Palestinian conflict in particular, has been felt most acutely in the context of international law and the protection of human rights. The UN 'Alliance of Civilizations' report sees the Palestine issue as

---

3 Putzel 2005, 5.
4 Grimmett 2006.

a major factor in the widening rift between Muslim-majority and Western societies. It identifies this as a – if not the – priority issue for resolution.

235 Although it is extremely difficult to attribute causality to the approach of some Western countries to particular conflicts, researchers consistently identify the prolonged Israeli–Palestinian conflict, the invasion of Iraq, and the continued presence of Western military forces there as important factors in the radicalisation of young Muslims, particularly those in Western countries. The Commission believes this needs to be addressed – and dialogue and consistency in action which conforms to agreed international standards is an important means of beginning to achieve this.

Engagement with and through international institutions, in itself, confers respect

236 A different sort of impunity occurs when powerful countries refuse to ratify, or, having ratified, refuse to honour, UN and other international agreements and treaties. Many countries are slow to follow through on their international commitments due to capacity constraints as well as for political reasons. There is, therefore, a pressing need for the world's most powerful countries and oldest democracies to show demonstrated commitment to this process.

237 The controversy over the treatment of prisoners at Guantanamo and Abu Ghraib has raised questions about respect for international law. The Commission believes that such incidents weaken the moral authority of the world's most economically advanced countries. Some argue it gives organizations advocating terror the opportunity to operate from what may be seen as the moral high ground, though in fact organizations that are committed to violence and extremism have forfeited the real moral high ground. The Commission observes that the outcomes are deeply damaging for Western developed countries and can permit terrorist and extremist organizations and groups bent on hatred and violence to gain tactical advantage in shaping hearts and minds.

Devaluing the currency of respect and understanding

238 A sense of injustice and unilateral invulnerability can have long-term consequences, particularly when they arise from actions which are undertaken by the world's most developed democracies. The effects of these actions are to erode trust between countries in various ways:

- They can create a precedent of rule-breaking that may be hard to contain.
- They may reduce support from other countries that no longer trust their integrity.
- There is evidence that they allow radical elements to gain legitimacy amongst a wider public.

239 If the world's developed democracies are seen to abuse their power, opt out of international agreements (such as on the environment), or act solely in their own perceived interests, it is possible that others will follow their lead. Individuals and groups must have a reason to trust in international systems of governance and see them as applying equally to all nations.

240 There is, in addition, a pressing need to respect decisions made by the people when they have been consulted in a credible way. Big power states are wrong-footed when they do not accept the decisions of the people as expressed through democratic elections. A particularly challenging case is one outside the Commonwealth – in Palestine. There, after demanding that all parties and groups submit to the democratic process, most Western governments refused to accept the electoral outcome. There is on the one hand, the need for all countries including the world leaders to accept the outcomes of free and fair elections, no matter where they occur, and also on the other hand, the need for elected parties to abide by the requirements of democratic processes, including respecting rights of other parties, media and open public discussion.

Respect and understanding to underpin change is embodied in Commonwealth membership as well

241 When countries have been suspended from the Commonwealth, it has normally been because they have been unable to honour the Commonwealth principle of dialogue and participatory freedom with regard to their own people. Thus suspension has been incurred where the military has overthrown democratically elected governments or where there have been serious or persistent violations of Commonwealth values.

242 But, significantly, it is not the Commonwealth approach to cut connections completely or to ask member countries to leave the Commonwealth family; when members leave it is normally their leaders' decision, as was the case with Zimbabwe. This is particularly tragic given the effort expended by the Commonwealth in supporting the people of Zimbabwe to achieve their freedom from the Rhodesian regime.

243 As is often the case in human relations, those who have been abused can become the abusers. The terrible violence being done to the opposition and many ordinary people in the country today, shows no respect for common humanity, the rule of law, or even self-interested economics. It is our belief that this is not because the Commonwealth way of working has failed, but rather that it has not been tried over the years with enough persuasion and persistence. The Commission acknowledges that efforts with regard to Zimbabwe continue, and must be strengthened.

Showing respect to regional neighbours reflects and reinforces multilaterist thinking

244 Deep feelings of disrespect and humiliation sometimes emanate from a feeling of how 'one's people' are being treated in other countries by other peoples and by other governments. In short, kith-and-kinship identity can become both regionalized and globalized. In searching for ways to re-engender feelings of respect

and understanding at a local level, the Commission believes there is also need to understand this wider sense of injustice – to understand why it occurs and how it can be addressed.

245 True regional co-operation needs to be based on sentiments of respect and understanding between nations in the region, whatever the size of their economy or their political influence. A partnership approach is one outcome. Greater understanding between partners who take different views is another.

246 Small, landlocked countries are particularly reliant on relations with larger neighbours, as are small island states on the development of good regional networks and sound policies that benefit them all. Island states tend to have certain vulnerabilities in common: to environmental disasters, to the consequences of climate change, to the international trade system, and to public health issues, including HIV/AIDS. Sometimes they have the added difficulty of communicating within and between countries because of distance (the collections of islands that make up Kiribati stretch over 3,500km).

247 These factors mean that these small island states must develop partnerships, based on trust, for developing shared beneficial strategies, pooling their human and financial resources and establishing priorities. They have a lot to gain from close dialogue and co-operation with each other and with their larger neighbours.

248 Regional grievances are most likely to arise as a result of economically and politically dominant countries behaving in a way that makes smaller countries feel like periphery states. This can occur whenever there is a considerable discrepancy in scale. In the Pacific region, Australia and New Zealand are the strongest nations in terms of economic status and also the largest donors to other Pacific Islands. For the Caribbean the US is the dominant regional power.

249 Powerful countries need to be continually aware that there are thoughtful and respectful ways to conduct affairs with smaller neighbours. They also need to be motivated to act in accordance with their awareness. Principles of respect need to underlie all relationships, not just high-level ones between governments, but

between the whole range of institutional and individual contacts that citizens and youth groups have with each other. Finally, and importantly, it means seeing small states as homelands to people, cultures and perspectives – and not primarily as potential problems, for example, as havens for terrorists.

250 Small states are integral to the Commonwealth's identity: as a diverse group of nations, 32 of its 53 member countries are small states, most of them with populations of less than 1.5 million. Small states are making determined efforts to pursue sustainable growth and devise coherent strategies for integrating their economies with the larger trading blocs and with new trading systems. The Commonwealth is supporting small states in these endeavours and is an excellent forum to emphasize the importance of all countries being treated with respect and as equals, regardless of the size of their economy, their population or their influence on world affairs.

9. The Way Forward

Promoting dignity and dialogue

251 The Commonwealth Commission for Respect and Understanding was established in response to growing concerns about systematic group violence in the world, and the widespread disrespect and anger that prepare the ground for it. Antagonism and violence along the lines of exploitable divisions have taken on a global character in recent years. They find expression in acts of terrorism against civilian populations, and in violent confrontations over territories and entitlements. Even some of the military strategies to combat terror have made their own contributions to casualties, including that of civilian populations.

252 A meeting of the Heads of Governments of Commonwealth countries is a good occasion for discussing and coordinating public policies within the group which has greatly benefited in the past from such interactions. It is also an excellent opportunity to examine the state of the world and the problems that the Commonwealth countries share with other countries around the globe. Aside from its territorially confined functions, the Commonwealth is an important global player in an increasingly interdependent world, and it has a duty to do what it can in trying to solve shared problems across the globe. This report, therefore, is concerned not only with what can be called the 'home affairs' of the Commonwealth (that too, of course, very importantly, but not just that), but also with the Commonwealth's role in directing attention to policy issues of general interest in the world, across regional boundaries.

253 One of the principal points of concentration of this report is the need for more active multilateralism to address shared problems in our strife-ridden world. The Commonwealth, with its considerable background – and success – in using multilateral means, can have a very important influence in pressing for that important approach. Indeed, the focus on dialogue on the basis of acknowledgement of the dignity of all people has been a quintessential mode of operation in the Commonwealth – it is even tempting to call it 'the Commonwealth approach'. There is every reason, we argue in this report, to emphasize, rather than renounce, this well-used approach in addressing the gigantic problems of peace and security that the world faces today.

254 Efforts to defeat terrorism call for a clear-headed understanding of the nature of contemporary group violence. It is possible to argue that the limited achievements, and sometimes counterproductive results, of well-meant initiatives to further peace in the world are closely linked with deficiencies in the underlying readings of the nature and genesis of global violence. Since the consequences, for example in Iraq, seem to have surprised and disappointed even some of the earlier advocates of these policies, the time for rethinking is surely now; all countries, irrespective of their past policies, should have a strong interest in this process. Even when past policies have achieved, at least initially, considerable success, for example in Afghanistan, the follow-up events have revealed serious difficulties that call for diagnostic analysis of what should have been done differently.

255 The Commonwealth has a long tradition of learning from critical examinations of its past policies, and the history of the Commonwealth is a testament to the importance of open-mindedness in undertaking retrospective scrutiny for prospective improvement. As it happens, even at the time when some of the more debatable campaigns were launched, there were also other readings of contemporary events – very different from those that inspired the campaigns – that were also defended in other quarters in the world, many of them within the Commonwealth countries themselves. Paying fuller attention to the wealth of understanding that existed then, could have, quite possibly, helped in a better-informed pursuit of world peace and

security. Efforts in search of peace can, in fact, be ineffective and counterproductive if they are based on a deficient appreciation of the underlying nature of global conflicts. The scrutiny that genuinely multilateral consultations and interactions can provide has pervasive importance and usefulness in determining the appropriate means for pursuing peace and security.

Conclusion 1: Use of Dialogue and Multilateralism

256 The Commonwealth has a well-established approach to tackling conflict and political differences, involving multilateral consultations and extensive dialogues, even when the positions held by different parties seem distant. In a world in which different people, despite sharing a common interest in peace, security and justice, find themselves divided by mutual incomprehension and scepticism, and sometimes even suspicion, the affirmation of the importance of multilateralism, with mutual respect, can help to create a more positive climate for toleration, support and collaboration. We attach great importance to the Commonwealth's role in placing constructive emphasis on the use of a dialogue-based approach to dealing with issues of group-based conflict in the world today.

257 More particularly, we urge the Commonwealth to use its considerable successful experience to contribute to mobilizing the international community, working with and within the United Nations and other international organizations. There is, we argue, a strong need for doing what we can to ensure that channels of dialogue remain open, that there are discussions to identify common platforms, that shared interests and concerns receive general attention, and that potential flashpoints are identified and addressed.

258 In the half decade following 9/11, global support for, and identification with, the US as victims of an extreme outrage has shifted undeniably. A large part of the general attitude has moved towards irritation, sometimes even hostility, in relation to the US-led strategy. It is instructive to examine why this has happened, and what could have been done to prevent it. A greater use of multilateralism and the policy differences that this would have made are natural candidates to examine in answering these

questions. The Commonwealth can play a hugely constructive role in the world today in bringing to the fore the importance of multilateralism and the effectiveness of a dialogue-based modus operandi in dealing with issues related to violent conflict.

Conclusion 2: Commitment to Civil Paths – Not to be Displaced by Military Initiatives

259 Commonwealth governments can help to promote a better understanding of the far-reaching implications of the general recognition that tackling global terrorism is far more than a security problem. Aside from governmental initiatives, civil society organizations can also play a constructive role here. The recognition that terrorism is more than a security problem is by no means novel in the world, but its bearing on the choice of policy priorities has been considerably eclipsed by the recent focus on military options and strong-armed security measures. Probing and robust policing is certainly very important in preventing terrorist activities. And yet terrorism has many complex underlying factors. Security policies, while generally important, cannot on their own, come anywhere close to solving – or even suppressing – the problems of terrorism. Many of these problems have to be more fully addressed through civil means, in addition to what the security procedures can achieve.

260 The recruitment of terrorist activists and the creation of a climate where violent deeds are tolerated by a large section of a normally peaceful population undoubtedly rely on impassioned advocacies of violence and emotional evocation of some special group identity, to the exclusion of all other affiliations. There is a need for much more dialogue and discussion on the richness of human identities and also on the need to avoid placing people in rigidly separated boxes, linked with religion or community. The cultivation of a non-denominational national identity can also be very important in providing political cohesion within a country, without denying the claims of broader identities that people may also wish to pursue, linked with continental loyalties (such as Europe, Asia, Africa or the Caribbean), or even the shared human identity that all enjoy. Policies here have to pay particular attention to the nature and content

of school education, as well as public discussion. The avoidance of sectarian divisions within a nation can be a very important component of the civil approach to peace, and the positive features of a non-divisive national political identity need, right now, a clear and ungrudging recognition.

261 The civil paths must also include addressing past – or present – humiliations, and what is widely seen as continued 'injustice' at the expense of the less-privileged parts of humanity. Extremism and radical search for violent 'solutions' operate through various alliances with those who have reasoned complaints about the nature of the world in which we all live.

262 We live in a world that has come to be dominated by military actions and violent encounters, where even those who are opposed to such methods tend to concentrate almost entirely on the counterproductive nature of the violent routes to peace, rather than on the positive and constructive role of civil initiatives. The Commonwealth can greatly serve the world, in addition to itself, in bringing the civil paths very strongly in focus for public policy across the world, including of course in the Commonwealth countries themselves. What is particularly needed now is not so much a detailed 'civilian manifesto', but a firm recognition of the necessary role of civil routes to peace and security. Very few things are as important today, we argue, as this general understanding and affirmation.

Conclusion 3: Addressing Grievance and Humiliation

263 Among the civil initiatives, particular importance has to be attached to those policies that promote the understanding and remedying of the underlying causes of grievance. In defeating terrorism, the perceived sense of grievances demands serious attention. When there is some basis for complaints, the case for corresponding institutional reform can be strong. The reach and effectiveness of that civil approach can be illustrated with the success of the visionary Scarman Report in 1982,[1] led by Lord Scarman in Britain, which

---

1 Scarman 1981.

greatly helped in overcoming the hostilities that found expression in race-related riots in 1981 in Brixton and Birmingham. Such riots have not returned in Britain since then, although similar ones have occurred elsewhere.

264 And when, as is sometimes the case, the confrontational perceptions are based on confusion or planted through extremist instigation, those misapprehensions would still have to be addressed through civil means, with good use of discussion, open scrutiny and a willingness on the part of others to listen to complaints and grievances.

265 Good use can be made of the experience of the Truth and Reconciliation Commission in South Africa. Its mode of operation included the need for the government both to acknowledge the perspective of the aggrieved, with detailed factual records, and also to make room for the burying of past hostilities when the inherited inequities are properly addressed in the present.[2]

266 The outcomes of these changes would have to be periodically evaluated, in a systematic way, since long-standing problems are not amenable to a 'once and for all' eradication. These evaluations should include tangible ways in which the perspective of aggrieved groups receives an airing and commands attention. And yet progress must ultimately be judged by the gradual elimination of the sense of grievance, both (1) through remedying measures, and when necessary, institutional reforms, and (2) through addressing perceptions of inequity with genuine interest and concern. While detailed plans would have to be worked out in the light of specific circumstances in each country (we have presented some possible ways and means to consider in different chapters of the report), the general strategy of going in this direction has to be clearly recognized and affirmed.

Conclusion 4: Political Participation and Inclusion

267 If participation is an important part of a multilateral approach to world peace, the critical role of political participation within the

---

2 Mani 2002.

borders of a country can hardly be overemphasized. While this recognition is hard to escape, its far-reaching implications often receive inadequate attention.

268 There is, first of all, the importance of a national identity that allows each citizen (and broadly even residents) of a country to participate in the political affairs of an undivided nation, as equals. The political sense of belonging to a nation need not be mediated through a person's religious or cultural identity: they have, of course, their own domain of relevance in other activities, like worship and the conduct of private lives and social intercourse. A national identity can be used to give each person an acknowledged equality in political participation, irrespective of religion, race, caste or community. Peace and the avoidance of violence within the borders of a country are very dependent on the cultivation of a non-divisive national identity – necessary for civil participation in the affairs of the country – without undermining the broader political or social identities that people also have across those borders.

269 The development of civil society is another area to which special attention has to be paid. While 'faith groups' are often well organized and well financed (sometimes from abroad), the non-religious identities, linked with language, literature, occupation, etc., have frequently been eclipsed by the increased role of religious politics in recent years. (For example, secular Bangladeshis in London often complain that their voice has been reduced both by the activities of faith groups and by the official priority given to religion over language in classifying the immigrant population.) The variety of groupings needs support, rather than dissuasion, since the diversity of groups helps to bring neglected concerns to public attention.

270 There is a delicate issue of leadership in pursuing the activism of civil society. There is much evidence to indicate that leadership can be very important in championing unpopular causes. Leadership can come from different groups of concerned as well as aggrieved people, including grassroots activists. Political leaders who draw attention to inequality and neglect may require special support, despite the worry that sometimes arises in the minds of the

guardians of law and order. However, vocal but peaceful political participation can have the dual role of (1) leading to a more informed making of public policy, and (2) removing discontent about not being heard, which can ultimately contribute to rage and violence.

Conclusion 5: Women's Political Participation

271 It is particularly important to pay special attention to women's political participation, since this is often seriously neglected. In this field, the Commonwealth has quite a wealth of initiatives and experiences, from which the different countries can benefit.

272 We have suggested particular procedures for making better use of the ties of the Commonwealth for this purpose, including:

- 1. the use of cross-Commonwealth measures of participation of women in electoral politics, both as candidates and as voters;
- 2. development of training and exchange programmes for women politicians, and aspiring entrants, to share experiences and lessons across different Commonwealth countries;
- 3. use of findings of research identifying particular barriers to political participation that women experience in different countries, and addressing the difficulties in the light of experiences in other countries; and
- 4. sharing of models of successful incorporation of women into civic and political life.

Conclusion 6: Contributions of the Media and Communication

273 A flourishing media can make a very large contribution in strengthening the civil paths to peace and security. Since governments are often tempted to restrain the press for one reason or another, the overall importance of a free media does need a firm acknowledgement. A flourishing media can make public discussion better informed, allow alternative points of view to be more fully expressed, and also help make the shared objectives of

the nation and the world more analysed and understood. In our chapter dealing with the media (Chapter 6), we have proposed a number of specific policies, dealing with both traditional means and new methods of communication, but in addition, it is extremely important to recognize the role of an unrestrained and flourishing media in helping political participation and dialogue, allowing grievances to be aired and addressed, and facilitating the hearing that public appreciation and complaints should receive.

274 This is not to deny that there are cases in which the media has been used to generate hostility to others and to promote violence. While some restraints would, thus, be useful and sometimes necessary, particular care has to be taken to make sure that the steps to do this are proportionate and balanced so as to safeguard the survival and health of legitimate free expression, which is central to the civil paths to peace and security. It is always best if self-restraint is undertaken out of a sense of professional and social responsibility rather than the restraints having to be imposed externally.

Conclusion 7: Education and the Role of Young People

275 In the civil paths to peace and security, it would be hard to exaggerate the importance of non-sectarian and non-parochial education that expand, rather than reduce, the reach of understanding and reason. We have discussed, in Chapter 7, a number of specific policy proposals that would help the Commonwealth countries to learn from each other's experience.

276 Commonwealth governments do, of course, recognize that young people are the inheritors of global change. This recognition has two different implications. First, it is important to understand the contribution of young people which is already enriching contemporary politics and social practice – one type of illustration comes from the use of 'YouTube', but there are many other types of constructive initiatives as well. Second, the understanding that today's young people will have serious responsibility for the future, which in turn has implications for policies that try to help the young

people of today to acquire the skill, efficiency and inclination to play active roles in shaping solutions to problems that they will have to deal with in the future. Nothing perhaps is as important here as making young people appreciate each other's dignity, despite their diversity, and also the importance of the creative functions of dialogue and discussion.

A Concluding Remark

277 This report has been informed by the importance of human minds in the pursuit of peace and security. This does not, in any way, underestimate the relevance of more standard thinking on the subject of war and peace. Military operations can, sometimes, be justified, and security measures are certainly extremely important in the prevention of violence and in the sustaining of peace. And yet it is the battle for human minds on which the successes and failures of terrorism ultimately depend.

278 Systematically 'engineered violence' makes effective – and often lethal – use of selected group identities with adversarial attitudes towards other groups, combined with the downplaying of many other identities that human beings also have, including the broad commonality of our shared humanity. In resisting engineered violence, we need as clear an understanding as possible of the ways and means through which the thinking of a large number of activists is influenced in a violent direction. The battle for the human mind is at least as important in resisting terrorism and brutality as battles to secure physical bridgeheads.

279 This should not be a difficult point to appreciate, given the manifest nature of global violence and terrorism, including the way the process of recruitment works from the potential catchment population, and the way widespread frustrations and grievances are used to build up a favourable climate for violence, with tolerance of violent deeds (often seen as 'retaliatory violence'). But difficult or not, the practical implications of the point have not received the attention they strongly deserve. Our concentration has been to bring out with clarity the implications of this general understanding.

280 Given the nature of the subject matter, some of our conclusions are more general than others, with recommendation of an approach, particularly the use of multilateralism and the Commonwealth's well established method of dialogue with recognition of mutual dignity. We have requested the Secretary-General to develop concrete steps that, depending on their specific circumstances, member governments might find helpful to consider. The Commission urges member countries to examine carefully these suggestions as developed.

281 While precise policies must depend on specific circumstances and vary from country to country, the Commission wants to emphasise the overwhelming importance of agreeing on some general policy priorities at the present time. This is exactly where the Commonwealth, with its history and experience of dialogue, multilateralism and civil initiatives can play a critically important role. There is something of importance here that remains very pertinent and useful for the Commonwealth itself, but which also has, we have argued, very wide relevance for other countries as well. The Commonwealth does have something to offer to our troubled and fierce world, in addition to having reason to reaffirm its own commitments and to making fuller use of them in working for peace with dignity.

Afterward

Original preface

When I was asked by the Secretary-General to chair this Commonwealth Commission, I felt both privileged and challenged. It has been wonderful for me to work with an extraordinary group
of exceptionally astute, informed and far-seeing individuals drawn from many different countries of the Commonwealth, bringing a huge wealth of experience and insight to our meetings
and interactions.

We recognized the difficulty as well as the momentous nature of the task that the Secretary-General had given us, in line with the decision taken in the 2005 Commonwealth Heads of Government Meeting, 'to explore initiatives to promote mutual understanding and respect' throughout the Commonwealth. The importance of understanding and respect lies partly in their intrinsic value – indeed they are indispensable parts of good living in peace and harmony with each other – but it also lies in their contribution to restraining and removing the group-based violence and terrorism that have become such pernicious features of the contemporary world.

Acts of terrorism and homicide are, of course, criminal activities calling for effective security measures, and no serious analysis of group violence can fail to begin with that basic understanding. But the analysis cannot end there, since many social, economic and political initiatives can be undertaken to confront and defeat the appeal on which the fomenters of violence and terrorism draw to get active foot soldiers and passive sympathisers. The process of recruitment is a battle for people's minds, making crucial use of turbid sentiments and crude reasoning. Cultivated disrespect of target groups as well as engineered misunderstanding of the ways of the world are integral parts of the process of instigating and sustaining violence. This is why the battle against terrorism and group violence has to go much beyond policing criminal activities and confronting military challenges – important though they are.

This report is particularly concerned with what we have called 'civil paths to peace'. The ways and means of pursuing these civil – in contrast with military – routes include a great many instruments, varying from intellectual confrontation of confused and flammable readings of the world (such as unexamined beliefs in the alleged inevitability of a clash between distinct 'civilisations') to institutional changes – governmental and others – that could make it easier for different groups of people to see each other as human beings with a variety of concerns and affiliations that need not be constantly at loggerheads with each other. There are also institutional pitfalls of which we have to be aware, for example a single-minded concentration on expanding the dialogue between religious groups may seriously undermine other civil engagements linked with language, literature, cultural functions, social interactions and political commitments that help to resist the exploitation of religious differences which begins by downplaying other affiliations. The battle for people's minds cannot be won on the basis of a seriously incomplete understanding of the wealth of social differences that make individual human beings richly diverse in distinct ways, rather than being lined up on opposite sides of one gigantic division – religious, racial, national, or whatever.

If the institutional changes needed for pursuing civil paths to peace call for clarity of thought, they also demand organized policies, programmes and initiatives with adequate reach. We have to understand, on the one hand, the role of economic inequalities, social humiliations and political disenfranchisement in generating disrespect and hostility, but we also have to take the concrete steps that are needed for making the hard and often exacting changes in the way the world is organized, in order to remove, to the extent possible, the deeper sources of hostility. Through investigating the linkages between deprivations – past and present – and the fomentation of disaffection, we have tried to identify the central concerns that could usefully guide institutional changes initiated by the respective governments, individually and jointly. But the civil paths to peace are not confined to governmental activities only, since the cultivation of disrespect and hostility can also be resisted by the working of the media, of political processes, of educational activities and other means of generating mutual understanding. We have also identified specific areas of concentration that can sensibly have priority in what we call 'the way forward', and we hope that this will be followed up by an action programme to be developed by the Commonwealth Secretary-General in consultation with member governments on particular policy recommendations.

Central to our work has been the Commonwealth's traditional approach of using multilateralism, making the best possible use of dialogue and discussion. Most members of this Commission shared the conviction that efforts to overcome the scourge of terrorism and group violence in the world could have gone much better had a more multilateral approach been used. But since there is no merit in finger pointing, we have concentrated instead on what can be done here and now to help make the world a more peaceful place than it currently is.

We have argued that being guided by the Commonwealth's multilateral tradition has enormous benefits to offer for all Commonwealth countries, and even beyond our borders. We live in an era of overwhelming global interdependence, and the Commonwealth has duties not only to itself, but also to the world as a whole. We have taken the liberty of discussing not only what we can do for ourselves, but also what we can present to others who share this earth with us, and on whom our own security and peace will, in turn, also depend. In this sense, the report is a modest attempt to present a Commonwealth-based understanding of the civil demands for world peace.

Amartya Sen
Cambridge, 9 August 2007

Letter of presentation to the report

8 August 2007

HE Rt Hon. Donald C McKinnon
Commonwealth Secretary-General
Marlborough House
London SW1Y 5HX

Dear Secretary-General,

We feel very privileged by your decision to appoint us as members of this Commonwealth Commission on Respect and Understanding. The mandate for our work was given at the meeting of the Commonwealth Heads of Government (CHOGM) in Malta in 2005, and we have prepared this report for you for presentation at the next meeting of CHOGM in Kampala, Uganda, in November 2007. We have worked as individual members from Commonwealth countries, and not as representatives of any government or any non-governmental organization.

We have tried to explore and investigate the content and relevance of respect and understanding between different communities and groups, including faith groups, and the wide-ranging impact of these attitudes for harmonious and flourishing lives within Commonwealth countries. We have paid particular attention to the way group-based violence and terrorism often draw on incitement based on disrespect for each other and misunderstandings of the way the world works. We have also discussed how these evils can be confronted through civil routes, making greater use of the social rewards of mutual respect and fuller understanding.

Indeed, given the prevalence of group-based violence today and the way it tends to ruin human lives and damage peaceful communities, we have focused particularly on the constructive contributions of civil paths to peace in preventing violence and in promoting peace, based on the powerful relevance of respect and understanding. The policies we have discussed are, of course, primarily for possible use in Commonwealth countries, but we believe they may have wider use as well.

Our work has been much assisted by the helpful contributions of our Consultants, Professor Shamit Saggar and Dr Sarah Ladbury, and we are very grateful to them.

We would also like to take this opportunity to note the wonderful co-operation and assistance we have received from the Secretariat, particularly from Alexandra Jones, Daisy Cooper and Matthew Neuhaus. Doing this work satisfactorily within the strict limits of a relatively short time would have been impossible without their help. We would like to thank them.

Finally, we would, of course, like to express our gratitude to you for giving us the opportunity to work on this important problem and for guiding the inquiry through your visionary initiation. We very much hope that the CHOGM will find the Report useful for its deliberation.

Yours sincerely,

Amartya Sen

John Alderdice

Kwame Anthony Appiah

Noeleen Heyzer

Adrienne Clarkson

Kamal Hossain

Elaine Sihoatani Howard

Wangari Muta Maathai

Ralston Nettleford

Joan Rwabyomere

Lucy Turnbull

References

Appiah, Kwame Anthony (2005) *The Ethics of Identity*, Princeton University Press, Princeton, NJ.
_____ (2006). *Cosmopolitanism: Ethics in a World of Strangers,* Norton, New York.
Clarke, Charles (2006) 'Global Citizens and Quality International Education: Enlarging the Role of the Commonwealth'. Speech delivered to the Royal Commonwealth Society, 15 November, 2006, London.
Estlund, Cynthia (2003) *Working Together: How Workplace Bonds Strengthen a Diverse Democracy*, Oxford University Press, New York.
Gregorios, Archbishop of Thyateira and Great Britain (2007) 'Submission to the Commonwealth Commission on Respect and Understanding', 7 February, 2007'.
Grimmett, Richard F. (2006) 'Conventional Arms Transfers to Developing Nations, 1998–2005'. The Library of Congress, Congressional Research Service, 2006. Available for download from OpenCRS: http://opencrs.com/document/RL33696/ (Last accessed 26 May 2011.)
Hossain, Kamal (1999) 'Question of the Violation of Human Rights and Fundamental Freedoms in Any Part of the World: Report of the Situation of Human Rights in Afghanistan' submitted by Mr Kamal Hossain, Special Rapporteur, in accordance with Commission on Human Rights resolution 1998/70. Commission on Human Rights, United Nations. E/CN.4/1999/40 24 March, 1999.
Malik, M. (2005) 'Discrimination, Equality and Community Cohesion', in *Muslims in the UK: Policies for Engaged Citizens,* Open Society Institute, Budapest.
Mani, Rama (2002) *Beyond Retribution: Seeking Justice in the Shadows of War.* Polity Press, Malden.
Moskos, Charles (1986) 'Success Story: Blacks in the Military', *The Atlantic*, 257 (5): 64-72.
National Crime Records Bureau, Government of India, Delhi (2006) *Crime in India 2005*. Table 1.8.

Plummer, David and L. Irwin (2006) 'Grassroots Activities, National Initiatives and HIV Prevention: What Explains Australia's Dramatic Early Success in Controlling the HIV Epidemic?' *International Journal of STI & AIDS.* 17 (12): 787–793.

Putzel, J. (2005) 'Globalisation, Liberalisation and Prospects for the State', *International Political Science Review.* 26 (1): 5–16.

Royal Commonwealth Society (2007) 'Submission to the Commonwealth Commission on Respect and Understanding, 16 February, 2007'.

Scarman, Leslie George, Baron (1981) 'The Brixton Disorders 10–12 April 1981: Report of an Enquiry'. Cmnd 8427. HMSO, London.

Sen, Amartya (1998) 'Human Rights: Is there a Commonwealth Perspective?' First Commonwealth Lecture, delivered 7 May 1998, London.

_____ (1999) 'Reason before Identity: Romanes Lecture 1998', Oxford University Press, Oxford.

_____ (2006) *Identity and Violence: The Illusion of Destiny,* Norton, New York and Penguin, London.

Stewart, F. (2005) 'Policies towards Horizontal Inequalities in Post-Conflict Reconstruction'. Centre for Research on Inequality, Human Security and Ethnicity (CRISE), Working Paper 7. Queen Elizabeth House, University of Oxford.

Taylor, Charles (2007). Winner of the Templeton Prize for 'Progress Toward Research or Discoveries About Spiritual Realities', 14 March, 2007.

Tevoedjre, Albert (2002) *Winning the War Against Humiliation.* Report of the Independent Commission on Africa and the challenges of the Third Millennium. UNDP Cotonou.

United Nations Department of Economic and Social Affairs (2004) *Social Dimensions of International Migration,* United Nations, New York.

_____ (2005) *Trends in Total Migrant Stock: The 2005 Revision,* United Nations, New York.

United Nations Development Fund for Women (UNIFEM) Annual Report 2000.

_____ Annual Report 2004–2005.

_____ Annual Report 2006–2007.

Bibliography

Alam, M.Y. and Husband, C., 'British–Pakistani Men from Bradford'. Joseph Rowntree Foundation, 2006.

Albro, R., 'The Future of Culture and Rights for Bolivia's Indigenous Movements'. Paper presented at Carnegie Council Fellows Conference, 13–15 June, 2005.

Alderdice, Lord, 'The Individual, the Group and the Psychology of Terrorism', *International Review of Psychiatry*, 19 (3), June 2007a.

_____ 'Introduction, Northern Ireland Assembly Companion – Rulings, Convention and Practice'. Northern Ireland Assembly, TSO Ireland, Belfast, Northern Ireland, 2007b: 1–6.

Appiah, K.A., *The Ethics of Identity*, Princeton University Press, Princeton, 2005.

_____ Cosmopolitanism: Ethics in a World of Strangers, W.W. Norton & Company, New York, 2006.

Atran, S., 'Global Network Terrorism', Briefing to National Security Council, White House, 28 April, 2006; available at www.au.af.mil/au/awc/awcgate/whitehouse/atrannsc-042806.pdf (Last accessed 26 May 2011.)

Blick, A., Choudhury,T. and Weir, S., *The Rules of the Game. Terrorism, Community and Human Rights*. A Report for the Joseph Rowntree Reform Trust by Democratic Audit, Human Rights Centre, University of Essex. Briefing Summary 2007.

Butalia, U., 'Women and Communal Conflict: New Challenges for the Women's Movement in India', in C. Moser and F. Clark (eds) *Victims, Perpetrators or Actors: Gender, Armed Conflict and Political Violence*, Zed Books, London, 2001.

Brighton, S., 'British Muslims, Multiculturalism and UK Foreign Policy: 'Integration' and 'Cohesion' in and Beyond the State', *International Affairs*, 83 (1): 1–17, 2007.

Brown, D., 'A Polyglot of Peoples: Ethnic Diversity and Leadership in the Caribbean Public Sector.' Published in Spanish as 'La Poliglotia de

Pueblos: Diversidad Etnica y Liderazgo en el Sector Publico del Caribe', in Oviedo, J. (ed) *Estrategias de Gestion Publica*. Republica Dominicana: Pontificia Universidad Catolica Madre y Maestra, 2004.

Castles, S. and Kosack, G., *Immigrant Workers and Class Structure in Western Europe*, Institute of Race Relations, Oxford University Press, 1973.

Cesari, J., *When Islam and Democracy Meet: Muslims in Europe and the United States*, Palgrave, New York, 2004.

Chaitin, J., 'Stories, Narratives, and Storytelling', in Guy Burgess and Heidi Burgess (eds), *Beyond Intractability*, Conflict Research Consortium, University of Colorado, Boulder, Colorado, USA, July 2003.

Clarke, R. A., *Against All Enemies: Inside America's War on Terror*. Free Press, New York, 2004.

Cohen, A., *Two-Dimensional Man*. Routledge and Kegan Paul, London, 1974.

Control Arms Campaign (Amnesty, Oxfam and IANSA), 'Guns or Growth: Assessing the Impact of Arms Sales on Sustainable Development'. June 2004.

Coussey, M., 'Framework of Integration Policies', Council of Europe, Strasbourg, 2000.

Cramer, C., 'Inequality and Conflict: A Review of an Age-Old Concern. Identities, Conflict and Cohesion Programme', Paper 11, UNRISD, October, 2005.

Davultoglu, A., *Civilizational Transformation and the Muslim World*. Mahir Publications, Kuala Lumpur, 1994.

Dench, G., Garron, K. and Young, M., *The New East End: Kinship, Race and Conflict*. The Young Foundation, London, 2006.

Eyben, R. and Ladbury, S., 'Building Effective States: Taking a Citizen's Perspective'. Development Research Centre on Citizenship, Participation and Accountability, Institute of Development Studies, University of Sussex, 2006.

Falk, R., 'False Universalism and the Geopolitics of Exclusion: The case of Islam', *Third World Quarterly*, 18, March 1997: 7–24.

Fearon, J. and Laitin, D., 'Explaining Interethnic Cooperation', *American Political Science Review*, 90 (4): 715–735, 1996.

Friedman, T.L., *Longitudes and Attitudes: Exploring the World after September 11th*. Farrar, Straus and Giroux, New York, 2002.

Fukuyama, F., 'Identity and Migration', *Prospect Magazine*, 131, February 2007.

George Washington University Homeland Security Policy Institute and The University of Virginia Critical Incident Analysis Group, 'NETworked Radicalization: A Counter-Strategy', 2007.

Gilley, B., 'Against the Concept of Ethnic Conflict', *Third World Quarterly*, 25 (6): 1155–1166, 2004.

Harb, M. and Leenders, R., 'Know Thy Enemy: Hizbullah, "Terrorism" and the Politics of Perception', *Third World Quarterly*, 26 (1), 173–197, 2005.

Heyzer, N., 'Women, War and Peace: Mobilising for Peace and Security in the 21st Century'. The 2004 Dag Hammarskjold Lecture, Uppsala, 2004.

Huntingdon, S.P., *The Clash of Civilizations: And the Remaking of World Order*. Simon and Shuster, New York, 1998.

International Crisis Group, 'Nepal's Maoists: Their Aims, Structure and Strategy'. Asia Report No. 104, 27 October, 2005.

Kepel, G., *The War for Muslim Minds: Islam and the West*. The Belknap Press, Cambridge, MA, 2004.

King, R. and Ladbury, S., 'The Cultural Reconstruction of Political Reality: Greek and Turkish Cyprus since 1974', *Anthropological Quarterly*, 55 (1): 1–17, 1984.

Koh, H. H., (2001) 'Preserving American Values: The Challenge at Home and Abroad', in Strobe Talbott and Nayan Chanda (eds), *The Age of Terror: America and the World after September 11*. Basic Books, New York, 2002.

Lewis, B., 'The Roots of Muslim Rage', *Atlantic Monthly*, September 1990.

Malik, M., 'Discrimination, Equality and Community Cohesion', in *Muslims in the UK: Policies for Engaged Citizens*. Open Society Institute, Budapest, 2005.

Mamdani, M., *Good Muslim, Bad Muslim: America, the Cold War and the Roots of Terror*. Three Leaves Press, Doubleday, New York, 2004.

McGuire, P. and Eyben, K., 'What Now? Reflections Report on a Political Education Project with Young Adults in the Rural Loyalist Community'. Supported by International Voluntary Service, Northern Ireland, 2004.

Messina, A., *The Logic and Politics of Post-war Immigration*. Cambridge University Press, Cambridge, 2007.

Mirza, M., Senthilkumaran, A. and Ja'far, Z., 'Living Apart Together – British Muslims and the Paradox of Multiculturalism'. Policy Exchange, London, 2007.

Nettleford, R., 'The Commonwealth – Reconnection and Renewal: A Voice from the Caribbean', *The Commonwealth Lecture*, Oxford, 2003.

Open Society Institute, 'Monitoring Minority Protection in the EU: The Situation of Muslims in the UK', EU Monitoring and Advocacy Program (EUMAP), OSI, Budapest, 2002.

Page, B., 'The Second Death of Liberal England', MORI, 2004.

Perera, S., 'The Ethnic Conflict in Sri Lanka: A Historical and Socio-Political Outline'. World Bank, Washington, D.C., 2000.

Putnam, R.D., *Bowling Alone: The Collapse and Revival of American Community*. Simon and Shuster, New York, 2000.

Putzel, J., 'Globalization, Liberalization, and Prospects for the State', *International Political Science Review*, 26 (1): 5–16, 2005.

Qureshi, A., 'Detention in the Name of the War on Terror: Violations of International Humanitarian and Human Rights Law'. Paper presented at the Bertrand Russell Peace Foundation Conference at the European Parliament on 20 October, 2005.

Ramadan, T., *Western Muslims and the Future of Islam*, Oxford University Press, Oxford, 2004.

Saggar, S., 'Boomerangs and Slingshots: Radical Islamism and Counter-terrorism Strategy', *Journal of Ethnic and Migration Studies*, 35 (3): 381-402, 2009.

Appendix

Written submissions to the Commonwealth Commission on Respect and Understanding

Advisory Board on Naturalisation and Integration, (2007) Submission to the Commission on Integration and Cohesion, re-submitted to the Commonwealth Commission on Respect and Understanding, 12 February, 2007.

Ahmed, Akbar (2007) Submission to the Commonwealth Commission on Respect and Understanding, December 2006.

Gregorios, Archbishop of Thyateira and Great Britain (2007) Submission to the Commonwealth Commission on Respect and Understanding, 7 February, 2007.

Nizami, Farhan (2007) Submission to the Commonwealth Commission on Respect and Understanding, 23 February, 2007.

Office of the Inter Faith Network for the UK (2007) Submission to the Commonwealth Commission on Respect and Understanding, 15 February, 2007.

Premdas, Ralph (2007) 'Multiculturalism as a Policy of Tolerance in the Face of Diversity', submission to the Commonwealth Commission on Respect and Understanding, 16 March, 2007.

Rao, Siriparapu K. (2007) Submission to the Commonwealth Commission on Respect and Understanding, 20 February, 2007.

Royal Commonwealth Society (2007) Submission to the Commonwealth Commission on Respect and Understanding, 16 February, 2007.

Sentamu, John (2007) Submission to the Commonwealth Commission on Respect and Understanding, 22 February, 2007.

The Salvation Army (2007) Submission to the Commonwealth Commission on Respect and Understanding, 12 February, 2007.

Tomlinson, John (2007) 'A Cosmopolitan Perspective'. Submission to the Commonwealth Commission on Respect and Understanding, 8 February, 2007.

Index

This book does not end here...

At Open Book Publishers we are changing the nature of the traditional academic book. The title you have just read will not be left on a library shelf, but will be accessed online by hundreds of readers each month across the globe. We make all our books free to read online so that students, researchers and members of the public who can't afford a printed edition can still have access to the same ideas as you.

Our digital publishing model also allows us to produce online supplementary material, including extra chapters, reviews, links and other digital resources. Find *Peace and Democratic Society* on our website to access its online extras:

http://www.openbookpublishers.com/product.php/78

Please check this page regularly for ongoing updates, and join the conversation by leaving your own comments.

If you enjoyed the book you have just read, and feel that research like this should be available to all readers, regardless of their income, please think about donating to us. Our company is run entirely by academics, and our publishing decisions are based on intellectual merit and public value rather than on commercial viability. We do not operate for profit and all donations, as with all other revenue we generate, will be used to finance new Open Access publications.

For further information about what we do, how to donate to OBP, additional digital material related to our titles or to order our books, please visit our website.

OpenBook Publishers
www.openbookpublishers.com

www.ingramcontent.com/pod-product-compliance
Lightning Source LLC
Chambersburg PA
CBHW070921270326
41927CB00011B/2669